WHAT I DIDN'T LEARN AT HARVARD

ROB REDENBACH

What I Didn't Learn at Harvard

ISBN 978-0-6488524-0-7

First published as *Waveman*

This revised edition published 2021 by

www.redenbach.com

A CIP record for this book is available at the National Library of Australia.

Edited by Janet Blagg
Cover artwork by Petro Morris
Produced for the Publisher by exlibris.com.au

"The over-riding charm of Redenbach's autobiography is that despite the dangerous locations and his obvious skill, the author is self-effacing as he teases out the fibre of human integrity."

Jane Fynes-Clinton – *The Courier Mail*

"I was absolutely enthralled by *What I Didn't Learn at Harvard*. Raw, honest and a lesson for all. It's bloody terrific!"

Anna Meares OAM – Olympic Gold Medalist

"As an SAS veteran and winner of the Telstra Business of the Year, I've lived by an ethos similar to Rob's. His book makes for a great read, but more importantly it presses home the necessities of hard work and, at times, a willingness to take calculated risks."

Scott Houston, CEO – Executive Risk Solutions

"*What I Didn't Learn at Harvard* is an amazing example of what can be achieved by combining a lifelong dedication to learning with fearless practical application."

Ben Pronk DSC – UNSW Business School

"Rob has a remarkable ability to take his readers from high intensity action to quiet reflection and calm – and in the process he challenges us to take the *right* path, rather than the *easy* one."

Mike Rolls – Author of *Ditch The Dead Weight*

"*What I Didn't Learn at Harvard* is kaizen in action, written by a man who measures time in heartbeats, learns from Sun Tzu and the poetry of Banjo Paterson and then applies his own lessons."

Dr Louise Mahler – Author of *Resonate*

"Rob has travelled the world showing Leaders how to lead in great times as well as in challenging times. His insights, ideas and inspiration throughout this book give the reader a real competitive edge in any business, industry or marketplace."

Keith Abraham – Author of *It Starts With Passion*

"*What I Didn't Learn at Harvard* is a fascinating story that feels like reading about a parallel universe. One involving guns, courage, fear and life and death decisions. But from Rob we can learn a lot about focus, emotional control and having the self-belief to make a difference."

Melissa Doyle AM – Journalist & Presenter

"Rob, through his book, powerfully illustrates there is life after leaving the military, a life that can be full of personal and professional successes, and the possibility of more exciting adventures!"

Kate Munari – Retired Military Helicopter Pilot

Breathe deep . . .

It won't last.
Nothing does.
You know that.
We all do.
And, yet
We hope
Or fear,
It goes on
Forever.
It doesn't.
So, why wait?
Breathe deep.
Jump in.
Get wet.
While we can.

RR

Contents

Los Angeles

Something moved at the edge of my vision. I turned my head slowly to watch a bead of sweat rolling down the deeply lined face of the man sitting next to me. It traversed the rim of his eye-socket and the broad, tanned cheekbone, gathering momentum as it reached the line of his jaw.

Sprawling low in the driving seat of the Buick, Jerry caught my eye and gave me a quick, quizzical glance. Twitching my lips into what I hoped was a smile I turned back to the windscreen and focused on my breathing.

In these moments – which I knew could stretch into hours – I needed the regimen of diaphragmatic breathing to help clear my mind, steady my pulse and give me the widest possible field of vision.

I sensed rather than saw Jerry give me a troubled look.

'I'm not happy about this,' he muttered.

'It's my arse, mate,' I replied.

'Yeah, but if you get shot, then it's my ass. It'll be okay for you. You'll be dead.'

I chuckled. I loved the dark humour of the guys in the FBI. I turned my eyes back to what Jerry called the vacant lot. The ground was scattered with the burnt-out hulks of cars, abandoned refrigerators and old washing machines, and the nameless parts of car engines which, rusting in the bright sunlight, were silhouetted starkly against the bright blue of the Californian sky.

The breeze was wafting a few tufts of wispy grass and straggling weeds and I made the conscious decision not to let my mind dwell on what might lay hidden there … broken needles, used condoms, dead – no, stay focused.

'You can always let me have a gun,' I said. 'You've got a spare SIG in the boot.'

'The what?' Jerry said.

'The trunk. You have a spare SIG Sauer in there.'

'Yeah, and that's where it's staying. I give you a handgun and something goes wrong in there, we'll have a bureaucratic nightmare on our hands. You getting shot is messy enough, but one of those clowns getting shot by an Aussie who's only supposed to be here as an observer is even worse. It would compromise the arrest.'

'Nice to know you're so concerned about my welfare.'

'Of course. I'm a caring guy. So, when this goes down you keep your Aussie hide out of the way. Way, way back. Way out of the line of fire. You hear me?'

'How far back do you reckon I should be?'

'New York would be good.'

'No. I'm going to be right behind you. All the way.'

'And supposing I get shot?'

'Then I'll pick up your gun and shoot the mongrel who did it.'

'Yeah, you do that. But don't say I said so, okay? It's not Bureau policy.'

I studied the rueful face beside me. 'It'll be fine, Jerry. No worries.'

'If I hear "no worries" or "she'll be right" one more time today, I'll shoot you myself.'

I laughed, turning once more to contemplate the decaying, windowless warehouse two hundred metres across the lot that was our target.

There was always banter before action, but the fact was – Jerry *did* have plenty to worry about.

It had started as a simple stake-out. The FBI had an informer on the inside of a drug deal planned to unfold in a plain panel van in the parking lot of a shopping mall. Bureau agents were meant to watch the deal completed and then move in; some of the fifty-man SWAT team would be in attendance as backup, just in case anything went wrong.

After I'd conducted my training session with the team, which had started before dawn and lasted until midday, Doug Kane, the team commander, had suggested I go along as an observer. He often did that. But within hours, both the place and the play had changed: the deal had escalated, with over a quarter of a million in cash expected to change hands; the location switched to the vacant lot. And, there were new players in the game.

'These men are dangerous,' Kane had announced.

I was sitting on top of an old school desk next to Jerry in the cramped, ramshackle, SWAT team briefing room in the FBI building on Wiltshire Boulevard.

'What he means is these guys are some of the meanest mothers alive,' Jerry whispered.

I had smiled, quietly impressed by the non-chalance of the men in the room; men I knew from hours of training with them to be totally professional, completely dedicated to their task.

'There are six of them,' Kane continued. He shuffled through his notes and recited a list of names that meant nothing to me, although from the undercurrent in the room it was clear they meant something to everyone else. Guys casually leaning against battered sports lockers straightened up.

'These guys are experienced, criminally aggressive and highly motivated,' Kane said. 'All are known to carry firearms, especially during a drug deal.'

Kane announced that the full SWAT team would be the primary force in the raid. SWAT would move in, SWAT would make the arrests.

'We'll take them on the vacant lot. The moment the van arrives we hit them. We won't give them a chance to react. Take 'em down before they get time to think.' He glanced at me from his perch on a desk next to the coffee urn, holding eye contact long enough to let me know he was serious.

'Aussie, if you want to sit this one out, that's okay.'

'She'll be right,' I said. 'I want to come. I've got

nothing better to do.' I was single and in my early thirties, young enough and dumb enough to be loving every minute of this adventure.

'Okay, but if it starts getting out of control, I want you to pull out. Jerry, that's your responsibility. If there's gunplay, get him out of there. You gottit, Jerry?'

'Yeah, I gottit. I'll babysit him. *Naw warrice, mate*.' It was a terrible impression of an Aussie accent, and funny because of it. We all laughed – including Doug Kane.

But by the time we'd arrived at the vacant lot Kane's sense of humour had vanished.

Although there was supposed to be radio silence until immediately before the bust, Kane had come on the radio, his voice distorted by the static. 'Heads up. The deal's changed. It's happening *inside* the warehouse. Targets are arriving separately; we can't take them in the van. If we want to nail these guys we have to take them as it happens. Inside.'

'This thing is turning into a crocka shit,' Jerry had moaned.

I could never make up my mind whether Jerry and the others deliberately parodied Hollywood, or whether scriptwriters tuned in to these guys and immortalised their idiom. Either way, I knew what Jerry was thinking. The same thoughts were occurring to me. Outside, going up against six armed criminals was exceptionally dangerous; inside, it was something close to total stupidity.

Yes, I thought, Jerry had a lot to worry about.

Which, I supposed, meant that I did too.

The radio crackled.

'Target vehicle in sight.'

We watched a dusty Trans Am bounce on to the lot and stop close to the door of the building. Two men got out, taking a moment to scan the lot. Jerry and I hunkered further into our seats as Kane's voice came over the radio.

'They're the targets. The short one, he's our informer.' We watched the men pull open the door and disappear inside the building.

About a minute later a white panel van slewed on to the lot, fishtailing slightly and kicking up clouds of dust. Three men piled out, rubbernecking the surroundings. They were wearing unfastened cotton wind-cheaters, just right for concealing firearms.

The radio traffic was frantic about the location of the missing sixth man.

Then Kane's voice came over the radio, sharp and authoritative: 'We can't hang here all afternoon waiting for him. We either go now or stand down. If he shows we'll take him. All squads wait for my order to go.'

Somewhere on the other side of the building Bravo Squad was readying to enter the building from the street, while the guys from Alpha Squad were finding themselves high elevation in neighbouring buildings to set up with their sniper rifles.

Pulling my Bureau baseball cap firmly on to my head, I breathed deeply and deliberately.

'Go, go, go.'

I was out and running while the final monosyllable was still echoing inside the car, my dark-blue Kevlar body armour with the big, yellow FBI across its back clinging tightly against my chest. Jerry and the rest of the squad were leading the way, their M16s at high port, their boots pounding the rubble; racing towards the building, desperate to reach the lee of the warehouse wall.

We made it, smacking into the wall with our impetus, all of us breathing in rasping, staccato bursts. The guys were superbly fit and I knew their erratic breathing was as much to do with the sudden surge of anxious energy as with the explosive dash in the heat of the afternoon.

We regrouped on either side of the battered metal door, taking a moment to calm our breathing as every member of the squad focused on his role in the team.

Jerry held up fingers, pointed, and made a number of unequivocal gestures. Two of the biggest guys moved to the door, one holding a large body shield, the other a short battering ram. Six of the others, their shoulders hunched, cheeks pressed into the stocks of M16s, moved into place behind them. All were wearing Kevlar body armour; the guys at the front in dark-blue combat helmets too. Jerry and the radioman, who had taken up position at the rear, had turned their Bureau caps around backwards. I did the same.

Jerry signalled, and SWAT Charlie Squad went

into Entry Against Armed Assailant mode. One of the guys at the front eased open the heavy door, which scraped and grated fit to bust, Jerry quietly cursing as, in an instant, the front men were inside, their M16s arcing, an extension of their field of vision.

Nothing.

I slipped inside behind Jerry, the radioman checking our rear. We were in a stairwell, stained, covered in graffiti, smelling of urine. A rusty iron balustrade and crumbling concrete steps disappeared into a murky gloom. We moved swiftly up the stairs and yet again I was amazed at how quietly big men could move.

Two floors; four flights of stairs; up in twenty seconds; no sound, no opposition; no hopped-up pushers leaning out and spraying our faces with a lethal blizzard of lead. We reached the second landing, where a passage went off to our left.

This was the moment of maximum danger.

Fifty metres of narrow passage with no cover other than an insanely brave guy with a big, bullet-proof shield. If, halfway along the passage, gunmen stepped out and opened up, there would be no place to go; nowhere to hide. And I didn't have a gun.

The instant after the lead man sneaked a look around the corner, Jerry signalled to move out and we shuffled tentatively into the passage, everyone's eyes riveted on the place fifty metres ahead where another passage intersected – the corner around which violent death might be waiting.

The squad moved slowly; ten metres, twenty, thirty, thirty-five … then stopped, muscles tensed, trigger fingers at the ready. There was a movement at the far end of the passageway, beyond the intersection. What the hell was happening? Nothing was supposed to be there.

A flash of colour; blue cloth and white skin; a face taking a quick peek around the corner at the end of the passage. Above the face, a blue combat helmet.

Bravo Squad.

I caught the unanimous sigh, the relief almost tangible as shoulders relaxed, trigger fingers eased off slightly.

We continued on, both squads stopping just short of the intersection of the passage on the left. Jerry moved forward and, after a flurry of signals between him and the boss of Bravo, a man from each squad peeked around the corner. Two thumbs jerked up. The passage was clear. Both squads slid around the corner simultaneously, each file of men hugging the wall on their own side. Thirty metres away, facing us at the end of the passage, was a door, slightly ajar, from beyond which came a low murmur of voices. The front men, assault rifles trained on the door, stepped delicately towards it, while I found myself the number four man in the file moving along our side of the passage. Whether Jerry was aware of my presence so close to the front I had no idea. But even if he knew, there was nothing he could do about it now.

The squads halted a couple of metres from the door. The voices from beyond it had risen; clearly the deal was not proceeding smoothly and it occurred to me that if we waited maybe the bad guys would shoot each other. But whatever was happening, it was clear the men in the room were unaware that the Los Angeles FBI SWAT team, plus one Aussie unarmed combat instructor, was about to descend on them.

Jerry raised a hand, the front men turning for the count. Five fingers.

Each man counted off to himself … five, four, three, two, one …

'FBI! Get down! FBI! Get down!'

Both squads erupted into the room, a score of men piling in, boots booming on the scuffed timber floor, their weapons trained, their voices bellowing that single, insistent command. *'Get down!'*

The noise bouncing off the bare concrete walls was shocking.

Three of the drug dealers dropped immediately, streetwise enough to instantly place their hands on top of their heads. One man thought about it for a second, but with the muzzles of at least four M16s in his face he gave up on thinking and knelt down. The last man, the one nearest me, hesitated, his right hand darting towards his open wind-cheater.

Luis took care of it. Luis, barely an inch over the minimum height for the Bureau, but the hardest worker, the most dedicated; pound for pound the toughest in the whole team.

It was perfect. Just like we'd practised in our training sessions, Luis shifted his weight to his front leg as his lead elbow shot forward, the gloved hand moving so fast it was no more than a black blur, the heel of his palm connecting with the point below the man's nose. The guy shot backwards in shock; you could almost see his brain blink in confusion. Luis closed the gap with the commitment of a leopard going in for the kill. Wildly, the guy swung a heavy right fist. It hit nothing but air. Luis had wrapped one arm around the attacker's torso as his other grabbed a large handful of hair. In the half-a-heartbeat that followed, Luis yanked down with one hand as his rear leg swept through and executed a takedown.

'Nice one, Luis,' I murmured. 'Where'd you learn that?'

Luis's dark face broke into a grin. 'Just something my mom taught me.'

'Yeah? That explains a lot.'

Luis laughed, the sound lost in the noisy cacophony of the room. Relief was everywhere, like a sudden leak of happy gas, the tension pouring out of the men like sweat after hard training. The room filled with controlled laughter in among the sound of the men on the floor being cuffed and cautioned.

The rest of the bust went without a hitch, after which we all retired to the local Ribs and Beer joint to celebrate the victory. About an hour into the festivities, Jerry disappeared to make a call.

Returning he said, 'My wife says to invite you over for a barbecue. You want to come?'

I nodded. 'Sure, I'd like that.'

Driving towards his home in Glendale, Jerry buttoned down the windows to let in the night air. It was a perfect LA evening; the sky indigo, the breeze coming in off the ocean cooling the city and wafting the fronds of the tall cotton palms along the boulevards.

Jerry sighed contentedly. 'You know, a lot of days I hate this job. Sometimes I wonder why I do it. And then, along comes a day like today and I know. Trouble is, you don't get that many days as good as this. But when you do … boy … don't it just feel great.'

I smiled in the darkness.

'I always wanted to do this job,' he continued. 'Ever since I was a kid at school, right from the eighth grade, I wanted to be a Federal agent and take down bad guys. Never wanted to do anything else. Ever. You believe that?'

I grunted, not really listening. Jerry's words had triggered something, a memory from another time and another place.

Alice Springs

Pretty Woman had just been released and Kathy could have been a double for Julia Roberts. The thing was, Kathy didn't *know* she looked like Julia Roberts, and behind her gorgeous hazel eyes flashed an abundance of wit and intelligence.

'How did you get this?' Kathy asked as she ran her forefinger across the scar on the side of my knee.

'An injury parachuting,' I said.

'Really? When did you do that?'

'When I was in the army.'

'Mmm, yet another thing I didn't know about you. Any particular reason you never told me you were in the army?'

'You never asked.'

In reply Kathy pinched a handful of skin on my thigh and twisted playfully, but hard enough to hurt. Satisfied she had my attention she let go and asked, 'Why the army?'

'It was all I ever wanted to do. Ever since I was a kid at school.'

'So how old were you when you joined?'

'Seventeen.'

'And when you left? And why did you leave?'

'Because of this knee. I was twenty-two when I

landed badly. They operated, but it was never the same again. By twenty-three I'd been medically discharged, which is a military term for being told to piss off.' I tried to keep my tone light, but Kathy wasn't fooled.

'It still bothers you, doesn't it?'

'I can't run like I used to, but overall I can work around it.'

'No, I mean it still bothers you that you were medically discharged. Doesn't it?'

I was silent.

She was smart enough not to push too hard, and changed tack. 'And after the army?'

At this point in a conversation I'd usually change the subject, physically leave or, in the right mood, bluntly say, 'That's none of your business.' In this case though, any one of those responses would have been unfair on Kathy. She was a decent person, and we'd been living together for some weeks now. She was entitled to know.

'I worked as a crowd controller. Mostly pubs and nightclubs in Melbourne, but some heavy metal concerts as well. It was a crap existence, but it paid the bills. After a while I saved up enough money to go to Asia. I ended up spending three years travelling through Korea, Japan and China.'

'That's a long time to be travelling. What did you do over there?'

'I taught English part-time and studied martial arts full-time.'

'What kind of martial arts?'

'No particular style. I just wandered from place to place, gym to gym. Sometimes I'd stay put for a few weeks. Sometimes a few months.'

'Did you like it? Sorry for all these questions, but I'm really fascinated. I had no idea about this side to you.'

'That's okay. Actually, I hated it. It was a hard living. I was hungry most of the time, I was always an outsider, and overall it was a disappointing experience.'

'Disappointing in what way?'

'I was searching for some type of light at the end of the tunnel. A guru, I suppose. I'd read about some great masters, people like Gichin Funakoshi, Morihei Ueshiba and Mas Oyama. But all I found were money-hungry charlatans telling me their style was the best in the world. In most cases they were surrounded by brown-nosing disciples who didn't know their arse from their elbow.'

'But surely you met people who were skilful, who were good at what they did?'

'Skilful, yes. Definitely. But skilful and good are not necessarily the same thing. In the end I got sick of all the tribalism and the hype. And I was broke. So I came back to Australia. And ended up here, in Alice Springs, working as a casino bouncer.'

'You forgot the part about hooking up with the hottest croupier in all of the Northern Territory,' said Kathy with a wry smile.

'No, I didn't forget. I was keeping the best part till last.'

Kathy laughed then said, 'You know, you remind me of one of those Japanese warriors. What are they called? Sam—?'

'Samurai.'

'Yes. You're a samurai.'

I shook my head. 'I don't think so. I'm more like the ronin.'

'Ronin? I've never heard of them.'

'Ronin were samurai who had no master. They were on their own; no masters and no permanent means of support. They were a type of martial arts freelance, wandering from place to place teaching self-defence where they could and hiring themselves out for dangerous jobs whenever they had the opportunity.

Literally translated, ronin means waveman. A soldier tossed by the waves of fortune.

She laughed again, a soft, tinkling sound. 'Some wave, Rob. Surfing you this far inland. Washing you up as a bouncer in Alice Springs.'

'Not sure I care for the washed-up bit,' I said.

'No, no,' she laughed, 'that's not what I meant, and you know it.' She appraised me and after a moment said, 'But you do know you could do better, don't you? Much, much better.'

I grunted. Another of Kathy's painful shafts of insight.

***

Kathy was the only good thing about my time in the Territory.

Kathy, and the sunsets.

Most evenings I would stand at her door watching the sun go down. I was never aware before that there could be so many shades of red and orange; watching, as the dark, desert night descended, the sky swept by a wash of pinks and purples and violets before dissolving to a lavender haze so fine I could almost smell it.

As darkest blue seeped into deepest black, I would go inside to change into my collar and tie before setting off for another night of aggression. Most nights involved disputes of one form or another, and although they weren't all physical, they were always heated.

It was a depressing existence. I knew I was lucky to have a job, but it wasn't much of a job to feel lucky about. The pay was terrible and the prospects were worse.

My working life was spent in a place where it was impossible to tell day from night: an artificially lit oversized bunker filled with polished jarrah tables and green baize, with garishly flashing lights and the moronic sound of crashing levers and tinkling coins, the atmosphere laced with greed and expectation, the bars noisy with drinkers banking on being winners, the vast majority of whom, before the night was out, would still be losers; some of whom would be turning ugly.

A few punters, the rare few, came prepared to lose a couple of hundred dollars as the price of a fun night out. Win or lose they would enjoy themselves and leave, probably drunk, certainly noisy, but definitely no trouble. These were the adults.

As for the rest – well – I didn't get it. Did they come to a casino expecting to make money? Had they never heard that the odds favoured the house? Or did they expect Lady Luck to shift the odds in their favour for the night? They might as well believe in the Tooth Fairy.

In the university of a casino floor, one of the first things I learnt was that the banal *lingua franca* of drunken threats was the same no matter where I was. I'd heard it all before in the clubs of Melbourne, although the first time someone in Alice Springs snarled, 'Your days are numbered, I know where you live,' they probably *did* know where I lived. That worried me until I realised that the real impact of any threat lay with me, the recipient, and not the issuer. Threats were issued by people who had lost control. In making threats they were acknowledging their loss of influence. In a way, a threat was almost a compliment – proof they were struggling to deal with the situation at hand.

How I responded to, 'I'll be waiting for you when you finish work, you bastard. I'll be in the car park, with six of me mates,' was my choice. I could fret about it, I could react violently, or I could give a dismissive snort and say nothing. I preferred the latter.

People who make threats are extremely stupid. The loudmouthed aggressors told me exactly what they intended to do, thereby giving away the most crucial advantage in any competition, but especially a combative one. Surprise. But usually, in the face of my silence and lack of reaction, the threats died and they forfeited all control of the situation. Even when a threat did translate into action and one of the loudmouths threw a punch, they would usually fall over their own feet. The people who issued threats generally lacked the technical skill to make good on them, and when, on the odd occasion, someone did know what they were doing, often as not, as I said, they had given away the game before they'd even started.

And then there were the hard cases who, drunk and losing, erupted into violence with little or no warning. These were another category altogether. They were not young bucks pushing the bouncers to see how far they could go; these were men who *liked* violence, who came to the casino as much for a fight as for anything else.

Although rare, the genuine fighters were hard core. And, as had been the case in Melbourne, once more I discovered that prescribed moves learnt in a gym against a compliant training partner bore almost no relevance to non-sport fighting. Martial art skills were definitely an asset, but only if you could adjust them to fit the situation.

It seemed to me I was constantly dealing with conflict, whether physical or verbal, and that much of the reason for this was the high-profile nature of the other bouncers. At that time the Northern Territory was the only region in Australia that didn't require police clearance for someone to work in hotel security. In practical terms that meant many of the people who I relied on to cover my back were steroid-pumping petty crims with a chip on their shoulder and an ethic of 'in-yer-face-so-don't-mess-with-me' screaming provocation.

This profile appeared to be the casino policy and was definitely the preference of my supervisor who, for the sake of this narrative, I'll call Milovanovic – or Milo for short. He was the biggest of the steroid pumpers, standing at one hundred and ninety centimetres and weighing at least a hundred and twenty kilos. He had livid blue tats on his thick neck, a long ponytail and a face that dared you to punch it.

I was not his favourite person, one reason being that I chose the low-profile approach.

'There's nothing wrong in being low-key,' I said to Milo. We were in the small room that served as his office. He had summoned me to deliver a lecture on how he thought I should do my job.

'Courtesy costs nothing and the adults appreciate a polite approach; some of them even comment on it.'

'Adults? They're all adults. They have to be to get into the casino.'

I sighed. This guy was infuriatingly thick.

'You go around the place being polite and the punters think you're gutless,' he went on.

'They can think what they like. It makes no difference to me.'

Milo's dark eyes narrowed. 'Bein' polite encourages the scum to have a crack at you 'cos they think you're scared, then me and the others got to come runnin' over to bail you out.'

'It's actually the other way around,' I said. I felt like spelling it out, even if I was wasting my time.

'The other way round?' Milo had a black gift for asking a question in such a way that it sounded like a violent accusation. His ability to blend stupidity with arrogant superiority was extraordinary.

'Look, the bulk of the dramas in this place are caused by people so off their face they just lash out at anything, but especially the nearest symbol of authority. These guys would take on a thousand pound gorilla if it were dressed in a collar and tie.'

'Whaddaya mean?'

'Okay, some of them think I'm an easy target. But they're stupid. I know they're stupid because they underestimate me, which is fine. I prefer it that way. It puts surprise on my side. Meanwhile, your high-profile approach attracts the punters who will accept a chance of winning a fight as compensation for having lost all the money in their wallet. They rarely bother with me; I'm not enough of a challenge. But you and the others – hell, they can't resist you. You're a magnet for shit.'

The porcine face glowered and the little eyes hardened with malice. After a bit of a silence to show me who was boss, Milo told me to get back to work.

I was pleased with myself. I didn't expect Milo to

change his approach, but I had at least given him something to think about.

But when I told Kathy about it, her reaction was surprising. She gave me a strange look.

'What?' I queried.

'You think that was wise? Talking to Milo like that?'

'Why not? I made a good case.'

'You may have made a good case. You may also have made a bad enemy.'

'Yeah, but I'm right, aren't I?'

'Sometimes being right is less important than being safe and happy in your work.'

The trouble with living with a perceptive woman was … well … she was perceptive. I had an uncomfortable feeling she had just made a valid point.

***

From what I've seen, beyond basic physical needs, people's wants occupy only two categories: a hunger for a sense of belonging and a desire for respect. Even here in the casino those hungers were ever present: the pot-bellied, middle-aged guy, with a young hooker hanging off his arm, strutting past the roulette table; the football team conducting loud drinking competitions at the sportsmen's bar; Milo scowling as he wanders among the poker machines looking for someone to bark at.

More conscious of the antics of Milo than of anything else, I surveyed the mostly empty room. It looked like being an easy shift.

From a voice behind me came a single word. 'Red?'

Even before I turned I knew I was going to see someone from my old battalion. For six years I'd answered to the nickname Red, the first syllable of my surname. I doubt if even my closest friends there had known what my Christian name was. If they did, they never used it. I was Red.

I recognised the face instantly. There was no mistaking the squat build and ugly mug, the skin pockmarked and welted as a waffle.

'Jocko? Bloody hell, what are you doing here?'

We shook hands vigorously. Since I'd been discharged this was the first time I'd bumped into someone I'd served with. And of all the people it could have been it was Jocko. My old running mate.

'How long has it been?' I asked.

His ugly face contorted in thought. 'Must be four years, or is it five? So what ya doing? Last I heard you'd been accepted into RMC.'

'Yer, well, I lasted for a day.'

'A day? That must be some type of record. What happened?'

'I was medically downgraded, because of my knee.'

Jocko nodded his head in understanding. And he did understand. He'd been with me the day of my accident. He was training for SAS selection; I'd been recommended for entry into the Royal Military College, Duntroon. We had run countless kilometres together. Invariably every run became a major competition. Sometimes I'd win. Sometimes Jocko would. Afterwards neither one of us would acknowledge the fact that we'd busted a gut trying to outrun the other. Instead, once we'd recovered our breath enough to be able to talk, we'd say something like 'Nice jog', or 'Decent stroll.'

'Bad luck, mate. You'd have made a good Rupert.'

That shocked me. Not only had Jocko never given me a direct compliment before, his view of officers in general was anything but positive. For Jocko to say that I'd make a good Rupert (slang for officer) was a real surprise.

'How about you, Jocko? Did you get across to the West?'

I had automatically slipped into the veiled, slightly cryptic speech that accompanies anything to do with special forces. 'The West' referred to Western Australia, where Australia's Special Air Service Regiment is based at Campbell Barracks in the coastal suburb of Swanbourne, Perth. It would have been simply bad form to come out and ask if Jocko was or had been a member of the SAS.

'Yer, cracked it,' said Jocko with typical understatement, 'but got out about a year ago. Needed a new challenge. Workin' in private security now.'

'I'd like to hear about that. You want a drink?' I asked.

'Yer. Rum an' coke'll be good.'

I ordered Jocko a double and myself an orange juice. 'So, is it a good life then, this private security?'

'It's okay. Better than the army. And the pay's

excellent. Plenty of work too; Africa, Indonesia, PNG. You want to give it a go, Red. They'd hire you in a heartbeat. There's so much work in PNG they'd have you even if you had become a Rupert.' He laughed again.

'So what brings you to Alice Springs?'

'I've been checking out a mine site over the border. Drove here for a bit of life.' He gazed around balefully. 'Looks like I wasted me time.'

We chatted for almost an hour. From time to time I'd see Milo glare at me as he wandered around the casino, but other than that, he left me alone. Jocko, once the grog took effect, was into talking about old times.

'You remember the recon we did on that island off the coast of Malaysia?'

'How could I forget?' It had been the first time in my career I'd loaded my rifle with live ammunition that wasn't a training exercise. Jocko and I had been given the task of trying to locate a couple of tourists who had been reported missing and our boss thought may have been taken hostage. In the end, it proved to be a non-event, but at the time it was hard graft with more than a few hairy moments.

Jocko gazed at me reflectively. 'Well … I never told anyone this before, but I was scared shitless that night. And you know what made it worse?'

'What?'

'You. You weren't scared at all. Icy cool as your fookin' orange juice you were.'

'Is that what you think?' I laughed. 'Well, you're

wrong, Jocko. Completely wrong. In fact, if I remember rightly, I wanted to smack you in the gob because I thought you weren't scared. I wanted to know how come I was just about crapping myself while you didn't give a toss.'

Jocko laughed along with me. 'Looks like we both got it wrong.'

As we chatted about the old days I was tempted to exchange contact details, but at some level I knew it wouldn't have led anywhere. Without saying it out loud we both knew we'd probably never cross paths again. We might manage a night out on the grog together, but our friendship wasn't built on that type of experience. Our friendship had been forged in countless hours of running, shooting, sweating and training together. Our friendship belonged in a battalion. And that was finished.

Over Jocko's shoulder I saw Milo gesturing at me from across the pit. 'Look, mate, I'm sorry, that's my boss calling me. I'll see what he wants and be right back. Okay?'

Jocko nodded drunkenly. 'No worries. I'm going for a piss.'

'What are you doing?' Milo demanded. 'You know you're not allowed to drink on duty. I could have you fired.'

I took a deep breath and said, 'What, for drinking orange juice? That's all I've been having. Check with the barmaid. Who, incidentally, has been doing good business serving the guy I've been talking to.'

Milo gave me a dark look. It was one of his

specialties. 'So why are you propping up the bar with a punter? You should be doing your job.'

'I am doing my job. I'm keeping an eye on the place while being pleasant to a customer.'

'Who is he anyway?'

'A mate from the army.'

'They let little turds like that in the army? Some bloody army. Anyway, I want you in the front bar. We're short-handed and there might be trouble.'

'Okay.' I turned to signal Jocko I'd be back. The place at the bar was empty.

'Now,' Milo snarled, 'not next week.'

I shrugged. 'Okay.'

Idiots like Milo are a dime a dozen. If they were to join the army they'd struggle to finish recruit training, but in their mind they'd be fast-tracked into special forces and quickly promoted to Colonel. In reality they lack the emotional intelligence to realise that leadership of others begins with leadership of self.

Whatever trouble was brewing in the front bar was inside Milo's head; the place was as quiet as a cathedral. I stayed there until my coffee break then went to see if Jocko was still around. He was nowhere to be seen, and I found myself disappointed.

I wandered upstairs to the administration area, past Milo's office. Two doors down was the security-camera control room. I knocked and entered.

Tim was hunched over a video monitor. He was a thin, skinny guy in his early twenties, totally besotted with video technology. Milo and some of the others gave him a hard time, even so far as bullying him – which, I thought, was really stupid. If anyone had real power on the casino floor it was thin, weedy Tim. It was his cameras that caught Milo occasionally selling pills to selected customers at the door; that detected most of the big rent-a-fists playing pocket billiards; that caught Milo's marathon nose-picking sessions behind a pillar.

Tim had the goods on all of them.

I liked the peace of the darkened room with its bank of silently flickering black-and-white monitors on the wall in front of Tim's desk. It was a sanctuary, an island of quiet in a sea of oafishness. Tim hardly ever spoke, leaving me to my thoughts and to my study of video-tapes of past confrontations.

'How are you going, Tim?' I said, sitting down at a bench on the far wall behind him and slotting a VHS tape into a player.

From the other side of the shellback came a squeaky, 'Yeah, I'm okay.'

I turned to the monitor, my thoughts on Jocko as I watched a rerun of the previous evening come up on screen. I'd been involved in an altercation with a drunken punter and I wanted to see what had happened and learn from it. The fact that the casino recorded the fights was one of the few fringe benefits of my job, giving me valuable insights into the nature of aggression.

Weak people, in the process of losing control, often reveal to you the very thing that intimidates them by attempting to use that weakness to intimidate others: the loud-mouth will get louder, the tough-guy will start to posture; the yuppie will sarcastically belittle an opponent. In the drunk's case, he'd shown his true colours by prancing about like a would-be sumo-wrestler before lunging at one of the croupiers. His attack lacked both conviction and skill, and the practical outcome was sloppy – almost comical. In this instance I had cannonballed in, grabbed the guy's hair and dragged him away.

I watched the video dispassionately, looking for where or how I could have done better. Something resonated in my brain, and I reran the footage. Yes, there it was. The drunk had made a slight move before he made his move, dropping his left shoulder before launching his attack. I had the feeling this would be something he always did.

I studied other recordings of confrontations. And when I looked for them, there they were – in every case, the person who made the confrontation physical had made a move before he made a move – a tilt of the head, a twitch of the shoulders, something.

When my shift finished I returned to the control room and spent an hour watching more recordings of old fights and scuffles. It was always the same: a person about to make the jump from verbal to physical made a move before they made a move.

I left at dawn, deep in thought. I'd been involved in martial arts since I was fourteen years old. I'd trained with champions, multi-Dan black belts and supposed Grand Masters. No-one had ever told me to watch for my opponent signalling their intention. Many instructors had spoken of being aware of telegraphed strikes during a bout, but this was different; this was about the transition from possible force to actual violence. I wondered what else I'd missed along the way.

I stopped halfway across the car park to gaze up at a sky streaked with pink, stationary in those few moments when the light was pale and tranquil before the hammer of the sun beat the land with a vengeance.

Back at Kathy's place, instead of crawling into bed beside her I sat in an armchair in the lounge staring out of the window. Kathy got up a couple of hours later and sleepily wandered in. 'You okay?' she murmured.

'Yes, I am. I'm fine. I've finally got it.'

'Got it? Got what?'

'What I'm going to do.'

She smiled and sat on the arm of the chair next to me. 'So do tell. What are you going to do?'

'I'm going to create my own unarmed combat program and travel the world teaching it.'

Her eyes widened. 'Wow. That sounds impressive. How did you decide this?'

'I think it's been kicking around in my subconscious for ages, but things happened last night that suddenly made me realise I could teach something different. Special.'

'Different, how?'

'The program I have in mind will be for the sole benefit of participants – not spectators. And definitely not an ego-boost for the trainer.'

'So what's different about that?'

'Kath, martial arts is an industry. It's like the weight-loss industry. Every man and his dog claims to have some secret technique, some trick, that lets people get superhuman results without having to work hard. But that's garbage. Mas Oyama wrote there is only one secret to martial arts: sweat. I believe he was right. I also believe the key to getting better results in anything that involves human interaction, such as self-defence, is understanding human behaviour; knowing how people think, understanding their drivers, their fears. All the styles I've ever tried were ultimately about physically showing off, making the participants look good. With all the choreographed moves we could have been on *Dancing with the Stars*. That's why I kept moving on. My program will be for people who train to improve – not to impress.'

'Well, I think that sounds terrific, but maybe people like glitz and glamour, it's what they want, so that's why it's on offer everywhere.'

'You're right, exactly right. But I'm not going to be pitching it at trendy fitness centres. I'm going to sell it to people who really understand and value unarmed combat: elite law enforcement agencies, special forces in the military.'

'But how do you get to sell it to people like that?'

'Simple: make it world-class. Genuinely world-class.'

She stood up and smiled down at me. 'I'm losing you, aren't I? When do you start?'

There was a note of sadness in her voice. I stood up to put my arms around her. 'I won't be going for a while yet,' I said, and tried to kiss her cheek, but she pulled her face away.

'No, don't kiss me just to make it better. I've always known you'd be moving on. I guess I accepted that from the start. I don't want to get all flaky.'

'You are something else, you know that?' I said, and held her close, until again she pulled herself away.

'Time I got myself ready for work,' she said, and headed for the bathroom. I really liked her, but ever since I'd left the army I'd been searching for something. I didn't know what that 'something' was, but until I found it I wasn't capable of giving someone like Kathy the commitment she deserved.

***

I knew it was going to be a long process if I was going to sell my program to special forces. First I had to devise the program and then I'd have to gain their trust and respect. For that, I needed to show experience – loads of experience. I needed to be in a position where I could put my program into regular use, in a place where I could teach it to other people.

I started carrying a small notebook around with me, jotting down key points I thought should be included in my program – and the things that should definitely be excluded.

I spent hours in the video room studying the silent, flickering images; analysing the body language and the move it preceded – a head-butt, punch, kick or even the throwing of a drink – the ubiquitous move before the move. I watched the other bouncers, noting the techniques that worked and those that didn't.

After a few weeks Milo began noticing how much time I was spending in the video room.

'It's my own time,' I said evenly.

Milo's piggy eyes narrowed. 'You need to watch yourself. Your six-month staff evaluation is coming up soon. You want a good one, you'd better think about getting on the right side of me.'

'Why? My job spec doesn't say anything about being nice to you.' I knew I was pulling the tiger's tail, speaking like this, but I didn't care.

'You'd better be, all the same. You want a good appraisal, you need to decide what it's worth – you haven't paid me a cent so far. If you want a good evaluation, I want fifty per cent of your next month's pay.'

I could hardly believe what I was hearing.

'I'm supposed to be *paying* you to keep this job? You expect *me* to pay *you* for a good evaluation?'

'You want to stay employed … and out of hospital … yeah.'

'It's not going to happen,' I said.

'We'll see.' He turned and walked off.

That night there was a major confrontation in the main bar. I had no idea how it started, but attracted by shouts and swearing I raced into the bar. It was ugly; four bouncers, including Milo, against seven drunken punters, and the watching mob was definitely on the side of the drunks. I waded in, well aware the crowd was turning more ugly by the moment. There were about twenty of them, shouting and hostile.

After a difficult few minutes we managed to get the drunks under control, ejecting them from the bar to garbled threats of, 'We'll be back you bastards. We'll fix you.'

'We were lucky to get away with that,' I said to Milo after we'd bundled the drunks outside the door. 'If that crowd had got involved we'd have needed to circle the wagons.'

'We'd have handled them,' he replied with his characteristic arrogance.

Charged with adrenaline I was feeling reckless. 'In your dreams. If that lot had got stuck in it would have been Milo's last stand.'

Milo turned on me, his face vicious. 'I'm sick of you and your smart mouth. Keep going the way you are, you're gonna find yourself getting a bashing one night and no-one will help you out. You get what I'm telling you?'

I couldn't be bothered answering and instead just walked away.

The following night I was on duty in the main bar when three of the ringleaders from the fight stalked in. I felt the hairs on my neck rise. Most people who promised to come back were never seen again. This lot were different.

I briefly considered getting Milo or some of the other bouncers to help me deal with these jerks, but I quickly saw the irony, not to mention the stupidity, of asking violent jerks to help deal with violent jerks. Instead I recalled the Chinese philosopher Sun Tzu: *Subdue the enemy without fighting.*

Walking up to the leader of the three, I stuck out my hand and said, 'Listen, I just want to say I was impressed with you last night. You blokes can really fight. Let me buy you all a beer.'

The three of them gaped at me as I called the barmaid over and ordered three beers. I watched their eyes darting back and forth between one another, trying to figure their next move. It was obvious they were on the back foot and I guessed they probably hadn't enough intelligence between then to add up to one average IQ.

As the drinks arrived, the leader murmured, 'Er, yeah, thanks.' He downed half his beer then turned and walked from the bar, followed quickly by his lackeys.

About twenty minutes later Milo stormed into the bar. 'What the hell do you think you're doing?'

'What?'

'Three idiots come back and you *buy them beer*?

What kind of bouncer are you?'

'A good one. Those clowns got bounced outta here and they didn't even know it. No fuss, no drama. What more do you want?'

'I've just about had it with you. You're on your last warning.'

'I haven't had my first warning yet,' I said calmly.

The porky face turned crimson and for a moment I thought Milo was going to hammer me. My jaw tensed as I watched for the move before the move. It didn't come. I was glad. With a supreme effort Milo turned away.

'That's it … that's it,' he snarled as he left.

I turned to the barmaid with a 'what's-his-problem' shrug. 'Now you've done it,' she said darkly. 'I've seen him in that mood before. Someone's going to cop it. You'd better watch yourself.'

An hour later Kathy was waving to me from her card table. I hurried over. 'What?'

'Milo's taken Tim out the back. He's going to bash him.'

'What for?'

'Tim showed the bar staff a video of Milo picking his nose.'

I laughed. I couldn't help it. Kathy wasn't amused. 'It's not funny. You've got to help.'

'You want me to fight Milo?'

'If that's what it comes to. Please, Rob.'

My heart sank. I did *not* want to fight Milo.

'Where is he?'

'In the loading bay.'

They were thirty metres from the door, Tim wide-eyed and pinned up against the wall as Milo, holding him by the throat, slapped him around the face.

'Leave him alone, you gutless prick,' I called.

Milo turned, letting Tim slump moaning to the ground. 'Come to save your boyfriend, eh?'

'Just leave him. You've done enough.'

Milo swivelled around and kicked the prostrate figure viciously. 'Little bastard was showing videos of me to the girls, having a laugh at me scratching my nose.'

I laughed; it sounded like a sharp bark and I wondered where it had come from. 'You weren't scratching your nose, you were picking it, you dickhead – that's how you jerk off.'

It worked. Milo turned from Tim and came charging towards me.

'I told you what would happen if you didn't shut that mouth …'

I watched him in the gloom. I'd seen videos of Milo fighting; knew his technique well enough; knew the move he'd make before he made his move.

And there it was, a shift to his left leg before feinting with his left elbow and then striking with his right fist. I came up on my toes and, as Milo made his feint I pivoted and lashed out with my foot, striking at his locked left knee.

There was a sharp crack. Milo screamed.

There are only two rules of self-defence: 1)

avoidance and 2) survival. If the first rule fails, the second must not. Unlike a martial arts competition or a boxing match, a non-sport violent encounter does not involve willing competitors whose aim is to accumulate points within a predetermined framework designed to deliberately prolong the event while simultaneously entertaining spectators. In a real-life violent encounter, once conflict becomes physical you have, at best, thirty seconds to deal with the situation. It's like trying to save yourself from drowning; if you can't do what needs to be done in the first thirty seconds, *more* time in the water is going to make the situation worse, *not* better. And if your opponent happens to be physically much larger than you are, you have even less time to imitate Muhammad Ali and 'float like a butterfly, sting like a bee.' Instead, you have to *commit* to going in *hard*. Scottish mountaineer and veteran of El Alamein, William Murray, was spot on when he wrote: 'The moment one definitely commits oneself, providence then moves too.'

As Milo screamed I rushed in and grabbed the front of his jacket with both hands and slammed him into the wall. I heard something crunch as I let go and seized his hair, crashing his face into the brickwork. Milo went down with a grunt.

Leaving him on the ground, I went over to Tim and lifted him by his arm. He was shaking. 'Are you okay?'

He nodded and whispered, 'I think so.'

I half carried him towards the casino door,

which suddenly crashed open, spilling a couple of bouncers, Milo's mates, into the gloom.

'What happened?' one demanded angrily.

'Milo had a go at Tim. Now he wishes he hadn't.'

'Yeah?' The man sounded threatening.

'If I were you I'd worry about him,' I nodded towards Milo, who was clutching his knee. 'He's going to need a lift to the hospital. I don't think he'll be walking for a while.' I helped Tim inside.

Less than an hour later the security manager sent for me. 'I don't appreciate being called out of my home on account of fights between my staff,' he snapped.

'Do you want to know what happened?'

'I've already been told. You attacked your supervisor and put him in hospital. His kneecap is in pieces, he's got a broken nose and a cracked cheekbone. I hope you're satisfied.'

'Actually, he was attacking me.'

'I'm not interested. Your money is made up to tonight. Collect it from the cashier's office and get out. You've got ten minutes.'

I shrugged. 'Sounds good to me.'

Kathy, when she came home, was full of remorse. 'I'm so sorry. I didn't think you'd be fired. It's my fault.'

'Not your fault, Kath. It was inevitable. And you were right. I had to help.' What I didn't say was that a part of me had enjoyed the showdown with Milo – not just because he deserved it, but because it gave me the excuse I needed to move on.

'Yes, but now the police may be involved. The security manager said you could be charged with assault.'

'I'll worry about that when it happens.'

***

I was awake at dawn when I heard the swish of tyres outside, and by the time they began banging on the front door I was dressed. I hurried to the door and opened it. There were five NT police officers, headed by a lean, grizzled senior sergeant. He was, to quote Banjo Paterson, *hard and tough and wiry – just the sort that won't say die*.

'You know why we're here?' he growled.

'Yeah.' I stepped outside and closed the door behind me.

'You coming quietly?'

'Yes. This is my girlfriend's house. I don't want any trouble.'

'Sensible lad. Now, give me your wrists; I'm going to cuff you.'

'No need for that,' I said as calmly as I could. 'Any one of you'd be more than a match for me if I decided to get stupid.'

The sergeant evaluated me with a seasoned eye, but accepted the challenge.

Without cuffing me they put me in the back of the police car and took me to the station where I was held for most of the day.

Kathy came to see me.

'It's my fault you're in here,' she said. 'I'm so sorry.'

I shook my head. 'Don't be, Kath. You didn't do anything wrong.'

'What's going to happen to you?'

'I don't know. No-one's talking to me. But the cops aren't bad blokes; it could be worse.'

Twelve hours after I'd been taken to the police station I was escorted into the senior sergeant's office.

'You can go,' he said.

I was surprised. 'What, just like that? No charges?'

'No, some runt gave us a statement. Told us what happened. Tried to bribe us.'

'What, Tim?'

'Said if we let you go, he'd give us video tapes of Milovanovic and some of his mates selling drugs in the casino.' The sergeant paused. 'Of course, we don't do deals like that.'

I detected the hint of a sardonic smile hovering around the man's lips. 'But you're letting me go, all the same,' I said quietly.

The sergeant laughed. 'And Milovanovic is being charged with possession and sale of drugs. When he comes out of hospital, he'll be off to court.'

A couple of days later Kathy came home from the casino with a message from the security manager. 'He says you can have your job back if you want.'

I wasn't interested. 'He can go and screw himself. It's time, Kath, I've got to go.'

'When?' I heard the tightness in her voice.

'A couple of days. I'll get a bus to Darwin and then I'm flying to Papua New Guinea.'

'PNG? Why PNG?'

'Experience.'

'What do you mean?'

'There are scores of security companies up there. I'm going to find one and teach them my training program.'

'You don't have a job lined up then?'

'No.'

'You're flying up there on the off-chance?'

'I flew here on the off-chance.'

'Yes, and you never liked it.'

'I don't know, Kath. It wasn't all bad. I met you.'

'Rob, don't tell me that.' She started to say something else, then stopped, her eyes beginning to well up.

'Come here.' I took her in my arms and held her close. 'It's not for a couple of days,' I said softly. 'Take some time off.'

After a moment she pulled back and gazed into my face. Tears were rolling down her cheeks. 'This is just another wave, right? Taking you up there.'

'I suppose.'

She laughed, despite the tears. 'I think maybe you're just a crazy waveman.'

'Yeah, probably.'

Port Moresby

More than two-thirds of Papua New Guinea is mountainous rainforest, yet what surprised me as I flew into Port Moresby was how unlike South-East Asia it was. I'd been expecting thick, green jungle and sharply forbidding mountain ranges; what I saw from the aircraft window was a series of drab, brown, treeless hills. But descending the steps from the plane was like dropping into a hot swamp; the place was simmering with the equatorial heat I'd known in Malaysia. By the time I crossed the tarmac to the immigration building I was drenched in sweat.

I checked into a hotel, found a local phone directory and looked up security companies. Jocko had been right, there were dozens of them. I photocopied the list and pondered which one to go for first – not that it really mattered. It was early afternoon. I bought a street map and set off on foot around the city.

The first two I found were hole-in-the-wall affairs and I gave them a miss. The third had a couple of late-model Land Rovers bearing the company's logo sitting within a fenced-in compound. I walked in and asked to speak with the owner.

Fifteen minutes later I'd persuaded Bine Menai to hire me as his Operations and Training Manager. The pay was a long way from great, but I didn't care. I was here for experience, not profit.

I started early the following morning. After introducing myself to the men, I checked the vehicles and radios, familiarised myself with the duty rosters, and accompanied some of the guards on their rounds. In the afternoon I received a report over the vehicle's radio that one of the guards had been attacked. We sped to his location, where an ambulance was already in attendance. The guy was in a bad way, his arm was fractured and a deep gash in his forehead was pouring blood.

The guard, although shaking with pain and shock, reported how he had been attacked by three men; the one who had opened his forehead was wielding an axe, the other two armed with a homemade shotgun and an M16 assault rifle. I saw him off in the ambulance before returning to the Land Rover.

Back at base I wasn't impressed by Menai's reaction to the attack. 'No big deal,' he said blithely, as if security staff were expendable. I saw things differently. Three thugs, had, without warning, attacked one of my guards who, with no training, had no idea what to do. These men needed to be properly trained.

I worked every day of the week, creating a program based on my experience and the ideas I'd formulated in Alice Springs. It was a process of trial and error. Some of my ideas were impractical, some were too advanced for the guys I was training, some were easily understood by one lot of guards but not another. Within weeks I'd mapped out a rough prototype that seemed to work, and already I'd started to see improvements. It was a satisfying process.

In the meantime I joined a local martial arts gym to keep in practice, and here I met Chris, a Canadian and a competent all-round mixed martial artist. He made a living as a pilot, flying supplies in a light aircraft into inaccessible areas of PNG. In conversation one day, I told him what I was being paid.

'How much? What are you, a charity? Listen Aussie, if Menai won't pay you a decent salary you wanna tell the guy to stick his job where the sun don't shine.'

'Yeah, well at least I'm refining my program. And anyway, I don't know if I'll get another job. Someone told me they were crying out for expat security people here and the money was really good. Well, I haven't seen any sign of it.'

'The money *is* good. Listen, leave it with me. I know a few people. I'll fix you up, buddy. Don't worry about it.'

The next time I saw Chris at the gym it was about a month later. 'Come and have a bite to eat,' he said. At a nearby hotel, Chris bought a couple of beers and we found a quiet corner. 'There's this security company,' he began, 'either the biggest or the second biggest in the country. It employs hundreds of guards. The guy running it is an Australian. Tough old dog, but he knows his stuff. He's looking for someone just like you.'

'Yeah?'

'He wants to talk to you.'

'Sounds good. Did he talk about money?'

Chris dug into a pocket of his bush shirt, dragged out a scrap of paper and pushed it across the table. 'He says if you're the right guy for the job he'll pay you top dollar. Australian dollars. There.' He pointed.

I glanced down at the figure. For the first time in my life I was staring at a decent salary. The job was across the ranges, in Lae, and Chris offered to fly me up there the following week.

Lae

Lae was a sprawling provincial capital of 80,000 inhabitants: a tropical mix of urban town-houses, encroaching jungle, tin shanties, barefoot pedestrians and ceaseless humidity.

We met in the open lounge of the Lae International Hotel. Sandy Warnock was a big, taciturn man who'd been in PNG for decades. He told me he had a lot of business interests in the region and wanted someone to manage his security company which, he admitted, would be no easy feat. The last two candidates had left within weeks. Within ten minutes he'd offered me the job.

'When can you start?' he asked.

'Well, I don't have a contract where I am but I don't want to just walk out on my men. Say a week?'

'Be here in five days,' Warnock told me. I wasn't sure if I liked the guy, but I was pretty sure I could work with him. His rules were simple: do good work and you kept your job; stuff up and you were out. That was fine by me.

Five days later Chris flew me into Nadzab Airport where we said goodbye on the patched tarmac, shaking hands in the bright, sweltering humidity. 'I fly here often,' Chris said, 'so I'll be seeing you.'

'Good,' I said. 'I owe you a few beers for this.'

'A few?' Chris laughed, 'You owe me a couple of dozen. At least!'

I started work immediately, doing what I'd done in Port Moresby: inspecting vehicles and equipment, liaising with clients and accompanying the men on their rounds. Inside twenty-four hours I'd come to the stark realisation that of the three hundred men and one hundred dogs I'd inherited, most of the dogs were the better trained.

At first glance the men looked the part – self-assured in their uniforms, confident, physically arrogant – but I'd been a crowd controller too long to be taken in by appearance. Although they looked competent, as security guards they were anything but. One of their most alarming features was their penchant for starting fights: not, to my mind, the ideal attribute of a security guard. Even more alarming, having started a fight, they almost invariably lost them.

From day one I started teaching them my program, and over time their performance got better. My program, which I called for want of anything better, 'Full contact partner-resistant body drill and combative strategies', was getting results; the ideas and concepts were proving themselves outside of training. The name was a mouthful though, until chance delivered me a very satisfying improvement.

After a theory lesson for the supervisors one day I collected up the papers on which my students had been making notes. Almost without exception the dozen guys had spelled the word 'contact' with a 'k' – kontact. That was all right; they weren't there for their literary skills. But then the penny dropped. There was something about the misspelling that gave the word a robustness it lacked when spelled properly. Also, in my mind 'k' added a connection to the term *ki* (life force). I liked it. That would be the name of my program. Instead of my current longwinded title it would be simply that – Kontact.

On the personal side, the knee I'd injured parachuting was giving me trouble, but I was teaching myself how to work around its limitations. I focused on what I *could* do, not on what I *couldn't* do. Things were going well. Of course, that is sometimes a sign that they are about to go awry.

Not long after the birth of Kontact, I found myself struggling to keep up with my work. At first I put it down to a cold or flu, but I became progressively weaker. I finally hauled myself off to the local doctor, a gruff Tasmanian and an old PNG hand who, after about thirty seconds, declared, 'You've got malaria.'

'I can't have; I take my antimalarial tablets every day.' Even as the words came out I knew it was a stupid thing to say.

'You always wear long-sleeved shirts? Sleep under mosquito netting?'

'Yeah, well, most of the time.' Now I was sounding like an idiot.

'Most of the time doesn't do it, son. Do it *all* the

time. You hear? Now this isn't a bad attack, but the next one will be and the one after that could be very serious. I'll give you some medication and you need to rest.'

I collapsed and was sick for three days, sweating it out in the tin sauna I called home. My secretary, Melanie, offered to nurse me. I thanked her kindly, but refused: watching me sweat and puke in the fetid air of the shack would have put the girl off men for life. I did, however, get her to go shopping and cook for me; with money in my pocket I could afford to buy good food, and that plus a little rest saw me on the mend.

On my first day back at work, one of the supervisors came into the office and announced, 'Boss, there's a mob of local boys out there, wanting work.'

'It's too close to Christmas, I'm not taking anyone on now,' I said. 'Tell 'em to come back in the New Year. I'll be recruiting then.'

The man went away and was back in a couple of minutes. 'They won't listen boss. They getting sparked.' I sighed and stood up. The malaria had left me feeling a little shaky and I needed this like I needed another attack.

Outside, just beyond the compound gates, was a growing crowd; a central core of young men, a lot of them drinking, surrounded by a mob of flotsam and jetsam from the streets. More were joining every moment. I hardly recognised my own voice as I called, 'Listen, I don't have any jobs right now.'

The crowd was restless, I reckoned they hadn't heard me so I raised my voice. 'Look, there'll be jobs in the New Year.' Somebody yelled out that they needed work now, the tone aggressive.

'I understand that,' I replied, and addressed them for a minute or so, trying to placate them; massaging the mob. I thought I was doing a good job until a rock the size of a golf ball whizzed past my head. So much for that theory. Another rock crashed into the fibro-cement wall of the building, then another, whanging off the bodywork of a car parked in front. Then one of the supervisors standing next to me screeched as a rock hit his face. Suddenly the air was filled with flying projectiles and the sound of windows smashing and rocks crunching into vehicle bodywork. Crouching under the hail I yelled at my men to help me shut the compound gates. Afterwards we all retreated to the offices where we watched the mob throwing stones at the fence until they got bored and moved off.

I stayed late to supervise boarding up the windows and to take account of the damage to vehicles before dragging myself back to my shack. The power was off and I lit a few candles, puzzling over why a whole mob would turn up demanding jobs, especially so close to Christmas. Then throwing rocks; hell, what did they think—

I stopped, scrabbled around for my diary and checked the date.

It was my thirtieth birthday.

I slumped on my cot and allowed myself a smile.

Just like a lot of people on their thirtieth birthday, I had got stoned. In my case, literally. It would be something to tell my kids. If I ever had any. Right now there wasn't much prospect of it. I was thirty and living in a tin shack, celibate, suffering the after-effects of malaria, my most valued possession a leather-bound edition of the complete works of Banjo Paterson.

It wasn't much to show for thirty years.

But then, I reflected, being a waveman, maybe that was all I could expect.

Chris turned up shortly after New Year with good news. 'Word's getting around about your training program,' he told me. 'The PNG police task force and the military want you to train some of their people.'

Within weeks I was training both groups in addition to my own guards.

In view of the training business I was pulling in Sandy Warnock gave me a small raise. Fully recovered now from the malaria, I was enjoying the work and getting to know some of the NCOs from the PNG army – these included some Aussie and Kiwi officers on exchange. They had their problems, some of which they voiced. Apart from not being able to recruit enough good men, they had difficulty feeding the ones they did have. There simply wasn't enough high-protein food to go around. That gave me an idea; I thought I might have a solution.

I went to see a client I'd provided payroll escorts for. The guy owned a big property in the Morobe Province that was plagued by feral buffalo. I suggested that some soldiers and I might hunt the buffalo; we'd supply meat to the army and a portion to the nearby villages. The guy accepted happily.

We set off at dawn; five pairs of two. My partner, Mark Kinnisopa, carried an army-issue SLR and looked more like a highland bushranger than an army captain. I was armed with a vintage Bren light machine-gun.

Four hours into the bush and the energy-sapping humidity was as crushing as a ton of wet cement. I felt exhausted; breathing was like sucking air through a wet towel and I had long ago ceased to sweat. For four hours I'd been checking every bush, reacting to every movement of the wind in the long grass, acutely aware that feral buffalo were fast and potentially deadly. The fatigue was taking its toll and I'd reached the point where I was seriously questioning the wisdom of stalking buffalo in their own territory with a guy I didn't know, who might be carrying that SLR solely for show; a guy who might never have hit anything he'd aimed at in his life.

And all to feed a few soldiers and villagers.

I was beginning to lose the battle to convince myself that I wasn't mad or wasting my time when three big buffaloes burst from the scrub eighty metres away and charged. I didn't think it possible, but instantly my mouth turned even drier, my palms and armpits suddenly sweaty. Six years in an infantry battalion paid off though; I aimed and fired a short burst into the chest of the closest animal. It stumbled and went down. I pivoted, aimed again and squeezed the trigger. *Click.* The Bren had jammed.

Wrapped inside a weird, misty euphoria, I watched the lead buffalo swerve, pick up speed and charge straight for me. Everything in my world slowed down, sped up, then slowed again.

As my body mechanically performed the stoppage drill – *weapon fires, weapon stops; cock-lock, tilt-left, look-in* – I also watched the beast closing in; I could see the hot breath from its nostrils, the plumes of dust erupting from its hide as it thundered towards me.

Suddenly, a shot rang out. The buffalo stumbled, almost went down, righted itself and, with all the tenacity of an enraged flesh and blood tank, kept coming at me. A second shot boomed, and the heavy-calibre bullet tore into the animal's heart. It died as it was running, crashing into the dirt.

As the third animal veered away Kinnisopa dropped it with a single shot. Turning to me and grinning from ear to ear he called out, 'You owe me a beer for that one.'

Just before I doubled over and vomited, I murmured, 'Mate, I owe you the brewery.'

Harvesting the kill proved to be quite a mission. I'd arranged for a hydraulic winch to be trucked in, but the terrain was boggy and difficult to negotiate. In the end we were forced to recruit a dozen or so locals to help physically drag the carcasses to a more accessible site. It was hard work, but great fun. A couple of village kids came along as well and together we laughed, panted and pushed until we were fit to burst.

When Chris flew in a few weeks later the story was still current. 'I hear you're feeding a whole lot of villagers and half the army,' he chuckled.

'The army gets fed and my client gets the buffalo culled. It's one of those win-win situations – so long as nobody gets hurt.'

'You're in deep with the army, eh?'

'Thanks to you. They like my program.'

'Listen, buddy, how'd you like to teach it to your own people?'

'What have you got in mind?'

'I know a few Australian army instructors in Canberra. I told them about you. They said they'd be interested in some kind of presentation.'

'Yeah?' I was excited.

'You'd have to give it in Australia. Duntroon. You know the place?'

'Yeah, I know it.'

Chris gave me a name and I got in touch. It took me less than a month to arrange a presentation at Duntroon to instructors from both the army and the federal police, and I devoted all my spare time to planning the demonstration.

I left nothing to chance, writing it out word for

word before memorising it verbatim, making sure I was word perfect.

Flying into Canberra I felt the same sense of coming home I'd felt returning from Asia, although it was a curious feeling to be back in Duntroon as a civilian. I was assigned a large room though I had only a small audience. There were five of them, but they were all highly influential.

I was hyped and ready to go; trembling with nervous anticipation like a racehorse.

My first major presentation. My first big chance.

***

From start to finish it was a disaster: an unmitigated, total, consummate failure.

A morning presentation, I started with, 'Um, er, good afternoon. I mean, no, good afternoon, no, um, good morning.' From there it went downhill. Fast.

Four minutes in I forgot my lines, made a guess at what I wanted to say, said something I recognised from the end of the presentation, carried on wrapping up the event before I'd started it, stopped, said something that wasn't in the script at all and then began mumbling incomprehensibly as my mind went blank and my palms turned clammy.

Nine minutes in a major sighed loudly, stood up and strode from the room, passing directly in front of me on his way out the door. I'd just lost twenty per cent of my audience. From the look on their faces I could see the remaining members were staying out of pure, heartfelt sympathy for another human being committing the public speaking equivalent of *hara kiri*.

The presentation dragged to its sorry end like a dying animal and I flew out the following day, wanting nothing more than to lose myself in the steamy heat of deepest Papua New Guinea.

Looking back on the affair, I realise I'd made the classic mistake of public speaking: I'd focused on reciting the words of a prepared speech rather than focusing on engaging my audience. In hindsight, wonderful thing that that is, there were so many things I did wrong in that presentation I'm surprised that only one person walked out.

When Sandy Warnock and Chris asked me how it had gone I fudged something about it going as well as could be expected and maybe hearing from Duntroon sometime. I never heard a word of course.

I got another dose of malaria. Soon after I recovered I travelled to meet with the organiser of a major agricultural show. The event was the highlight of Lae's calendar, and in view of the fact that it would feature two big beer tents, I recommended the client hire at least sixty guards and twenty dogs. The client, more concerned about maximising his beer sales, opted for twenty guards and ten dogs. It wasn't enough.

The tents were packed and by mid-afternoon

almost all the men were drunk. A fight broke out between two rival groups. My men, though outnumbered, went in with the dogs to break it up.

In the ensuing melee two of my guards were badly injured and had to be taken to hospital. One of them was a dog handler and his dog, Zeus, a large, aggressive German shepherd, now minus its master, was uncontrollable. The dog had been secured in a wire-fenced kennel where it was now being taunted by a bunch of drunks. The racket of the dog leaping at the wire and barking maniacally, along with the drunks laughing and bellowing, was deafening. The client demanded I get the dog out of there.

I eyed the snarling animal: hackles raised, eyes bulging, its big yellow teeth bared. In the absence of its master, all human beings were its enemy. And to get to it, I had to crawl down a long, tunnel-like flue into the kennel. I would be entering the animal's personal space, on all fours.

One of my senior guards reckoned it was impossible to get to the dog and suggested we shoot it. I wasn't keen on that idea; the German shepherd was a valuable asset, and anyway it wasn't the dog's fault it was out of control. If I had my way I'd rather shoot the bastards taunting it.

I chose to believe it was *possible* to restrain and control the dog. I thought about Alice Springs where I'd restrained and controlled a lot of humanoid animals successfully. The principles had to be the same. I would have to take a hit – or in this case a bite – my only choice being where the bite would be. I pulled off my shirt and wrapped it around my left forearm, dragged open the door of the tunnel, crouched down, and set off at a crawl towards Zeus.

The crowd outside the wire went wild, screaming at the dog to attack me. As far as they were concerned this was the ultimate spectator sport. The dog backed up, its barking reaching a new level of frenzy. As I crawled I told myself repeatedly that the dog was more frightened of me than I was of it and that it was *possible* for me to come out of this in one piece. I could do this, I assured myself, and hoped it was true.

Just at the moment I judged the dog was about to attack I shot my forearm out. Zeus hurled himself at it and bit down. Even with the protection of the shirt, it hurt like hell, but at least it didn't draw blood. I slammed my fist into the side of the dog's head. Zeus yelped and staggered sideways, but didn't go down. The crowd was instantly silent, waiting with bated breath for the next attack.

It never came. The German shepherd whimpered, sank to its haunches and flattened its ears. Its body language was clear. In the power structure of the animal's social hierarchy Zeus had just promoted me to top dog. I backed down the tunnel, the dog following me peacefully, and emerged to uproarious clapping and cheering. Handing the dog over to one of my guards I looked at the crowd. The same people who had been baying for my blood were now cheering me. Such is the nature of a mob. As fickle as the wind.

***

Shortly after the incident with Zeus I rented a small bungalow on a nearby coconut plantation. I needed some space of my own. With the bungalow came a television, something I had neither seen nor missed since arriving in Lae. For a novelty I turned on CNN and watched the news. It was full of South Africa.

After twenty-seven years as a prisoner on Robben Island, Nelson Mandela had been released and was about to lead South Africa into its first truly democratic election. Mandela was certain to become the country's first democratically elected president.

I wasn't inclined to hero-worship; I'd had that knocked out of me travelling over half of Asia in search of a 'guru' worthy of the title. I didn't believe in gurus. And I doubted there were many real heroes. But if there were, then Mandela had to be counted in the front rank.

I watched the news whenever I was able, while reading everything I could get my hands on about South Africa. Gradually I realised that I wanted to be a part of what was happening out there.

Slowly, it came to me that I had something to offer. Kontact. I would travel to South Africa and teach my program to the police and the security services.

Maybe even Nelson Mandela's bodyguards, if I could. Teach them to be better bodyguards, and in so doing gain a whole new degree of respect and credibility for my program.

It was a great plan. At least, I thought so.

Pretoria

'You want to what?' Chris's tone held that special mix of sympathy and condescension people reserve for half-wits. I told him again of my plans to teach Kontact in South Africa. He laughed. 'Man, you're nuts. Mandela is one of the most famous people in the world. His security will be in the hands of pros. There's no way an Australian civilian is going to get within spitting distance of someone like that.'

Chris's attitude puzzled me. I guessed feedback from my disastrous presentation in Canberra had filtered back to him, but there seemed to be something more. At first I couldn't work it out, but eventually the only thing I could conclude was that he was envious of my ambition. Like me, Chris had washed up in PNG as a bit of a misfit. Yes, he was making good money, but he was living pay-packet to pay-packet. When he wasn't working, and when he wasn't in the gym, he was drinking. In the time I'd known him, he'd moved from a heavy focus on the gym to a heavy focus on drinking. I wanted more than that type of pointless existence and I think Chris saw my desire to move on to something better as a personal insult.

In trying to 'talk reason' into me he said, 'You

don't know anyone in South Africa. How on earth are you going to even get your foot in the door?' This question had been preoccupying me for weeks. I'd called the South African consulate asking for a list of the country's police stations and been told, none too politely, to shove off. I had better luck when I dialled the international operator and asked for the number of the Soweto police station.

I needed a story and after a day or so came up with one. I called Soweto, telling the duty officer who answered the phone I was an Australian journalist doing a story on how tough South African front-line cops had it in comparison to their Australian counterparts. After a few minutes the duty officer warmed to the story and the next day faxed me the complete list of every police station, prison and military outfit in South Africa. I put together a mailing campaign outlining the benefits of my training program and sent brochures and covering letters off to more than seven hundred addresses. Seven hundred and twelve to be precise.

Eight weeks later I'd received the grand total of two replies, both informing me that South African trainers were the best in the world, and that anyway, no foreigner could be involved in the security of South Africa's politicians.

It was all the encouragement I needed. Two contacts had turned me down – which meant that seven hundred and ten hadn't. The fact that they didn't immediately grasp the value of Kontact wasn't enough to put me off. I *knew* it worked.

I gave notice to Sandy Warnock, who wasn't happy. I did nothing to soften his mood; I didn't want to feel that if things didn't work out I could come back to the job in PNG. This, I decided, was a time for burning my bridges.

I landed at Johannesburg International and hitchhiked the fifty kilometres to Pretoria, immediately noticing from the cab of the truck how much I liked the look and feel of the country. It was more than the cloudless blue sky that appealed to me: there was a vibrancy, an expectation that something exciting was just a heartbeat away.

With my list of addresses I walked into one of Pretoria's police stations and asked to see the commander. The man who emerged was a big Afrikaner; irritated and scowling, he was the archetypal apartheid cop. I offered my hand to shake his. He looked at me as if I had leprosy. Folding his arms tightly across his large chest, he grumbled something in a language I'd never heard before. Afrikaans sounded a bit like German, maybe Dutch.

'G'day,' I said. 'I've developed an unarmed combat program I'd like to teach to South African security specialists.' The cop grunted. The action seemed to cause him pain.

'Actually, I've really been inspired by the example of Nelson Mandela. The guy spends twenty-seven years in prison, comes out, becomes the most powerful person in the country and he's got the courage *not* to seek revenge. Isn't that incredible?'

The cop, starting to turn an intriguing shade of purple, seemed disinclined to agree with me.

'Anyway, what I'd like to do is train the bodyguards of Nelson Mandela and in the process make them better bodyguards.'

I waited for a response from the cop. There was an awkward silence. Finally, he exploded into life. In heavily accented English he raged, 'You can't teach us anything. We're the best in the world. What would some Australian know about our country? And we don't have any money to pay you for training and even if we did we wouldn't pay you because we are the best in the world.' In among the ranting I kept catching the word *voetsek*. I had no idea what it meant, except that clearly it wasn't complimentary. The commander told me to get out.

It wasn't a promising start, and it turned out to be typical of my next two months in South Africa. I crisscrossed the country, visiting police, prison and military units at which my reception was almost invariably the same; it was as if someone had written the script. I heard the word *rooinek* often and learnt it meant foreigner. That made me smile. In Korea they'd called me *meguk* and in Japan *gaijin*. I don't know what they'd called me in PNG; with several hundred languages it could have been a lot of things. But there were worse things than being called a foreigner, and anyway, I was a foreigner.

My experience so far had been one of fierce resistance, xenophobia and raw racism. And I was running out of money. After nine weeks without a sniff of interest I calculated I had funds for about one more week, ten days at most. I'd left my number everywhere, but the mobile phone I'd purchased when I arrived in the country had only rung once – and that was when I'd called myself from a payphone to make sure the thing was actually working.

I was staying in a sleazy motel in Cape Town when it rang a second time. I was so shocked I fumbled, nearly dropped it and was flustered when I answered, 'Hello.'

The voice at the other end was anything but flustered. 'This is Warrant Officer Albertus Wessels. I've heard about your unarmed combat. I want to set up a demonstration.'

Again, I almost dropped the phone. Trying to sound cool and businesslike I said, 'Okay, where?'

'Soweto. The commander there will listen to you, and if he likes what you have to say he'll arrange a demo. That okay with you?'

'Sure. When?'

'Day after tomorrow. If they like it in Soweto we'll maybe try it elsewhere. But no promises.'

I wrote down the details. 'Will you be there?'

'No, but I'll get a report.' The line went dead.

I gazed at the phone. I liked the sound of Albertus Wessels. No bureaucratic bumbling with this guy. He was prepared to give Kontact a shot. Now it was down to me.

At Soweto I saw the District Commander, the

highest rank I'd so far managed to see. He listened to my presentation without a word, then asked for a physical demo, which he set up with two of his instructors. They were both big, and reasonably skilled, but they followed set moves that made them predictable and relatively easy to handle.

Rather than allow them to operate within the normal parameters of orthodox training – where light sparring or isolated practice of very specific fixed techniques (such as wristlocks, pressure-point manipulation, etc) is the norm – I conducted the demo in intense thirty-second bursts. Each burst involved free-flowing, unchoreographed partner-resistance drills that addressed what I called the Jigsaw of Self-Defence.

In just a few minutes I was able to highlight the need for good balance, accuracy in target selection, power generation and a practical understanding of how to deal with multiple opponents without being influenced by the utter nonsense of a Jackie Chan movie. Wessels called me the following day.

'Soweto liked your demo,' he said. 'You'd better come up here so we can talk face to face.' Wessels was at a station in the far north of the Transvaal. By that stage I'd been living on oranges and biltong for a week; I spent the last of my money on the bus fare.

I took to Wessels from the outset. In person he was genuinely friendly and from his questions showed he was keen to learn about Kontact. But the main thing I liked about him was his quiet air of confidence; this guy had seen a lot of combat in Angola; he was a veteran with extensive operational experience who didn't feel the need to impress anyone. He spoke quietly and acted modestly. The guy was also a miracle worker. After a day together and a lot of phone calls he managed to get funding for a trial course of Kontact. He also gave me my first taste of South African hospitality, inviting me to stay with his family for the duration of the course.

***

Twenty guys stood before me on the first morning. By mid-morning three had dropped out – Kontact was too tough for them. Training in anaerobically intense thirty-second bursts is not for everyone – and it is especially not for unfit slobs who believe arrogance and ignorance are a substitute for effort and hard work. Two more dropped out in the afternoon, and the following day I dismissed another three who were little more than oxygen thieves. Twelve people finished the course, out of which I intended awarding certificates to three.

Sitting behind his desk in his office Wessels chuckled. 'You know, here in South Africa everyone who finishes a course gets a certificate. You're going to have nine very unhappy policemen out there.'

'I expect I will, but I want this certificate to have real value.'

'Show me the list,' Wessels said.

I pushed it across the desk. Wessels pointed out two names. 'Why didn't these two pass?'

'They're both fit and fast, but they're also closed-minded; they don't want to try anything new.'

Wessels laughed. 'Well, the first one is a national martial arts champion. And the other one is a brigadier's son. Both these guys are legends in their own lunchtimes. I'm going to enjoy seeing their reaction when you tell them they didn't make it.'

Both men were plain bloody angry. After the awards ceremony they cornered me and told me I was a bastard and that I'd never teach in South Africa again. I repeated what they'd said to Wessels who smiled. 'Well, I don't know about the first part, but they're wrong about the second. I'm setting up another course for two weeks' time.'

'That's great. By the way, what does *bliksem rooinek* mean?'

Wessels laughed again. 'It means a foreigner who's in need of a good thrashing.'

My policy of maintaining perceived value, of creating a cadre of Kontact certificate holders, paid off almost immediately. Those who received certificates returned to their units to talk up the program with pride and enthusiasm. Some of those who failed asked to return for a subsequent course. The certificate and what it symbolised became valuable, its value enhanced by its scarcity, its scarcity a function of the enormous effort required to obtain it. Word spread quickly that only the best possessed a Kontact certificate, and even I was amazed at the exponential growth of my program.

Six months later, living in a small, pleasant apartment in Pretoria, I had delivered training to the South African Army, Navy, Police, Prison Service, Special Task Force, and, best of all, to instructors of the Presidential Protection Unit of Nelson Mandela.

Along the way I'd made some good friends. Albertus Wessels was now Wessie, friend and supporter. We also became neighbours after Wessie was promoted to Captain in the Police National Training HQ in Pretoria. Another supporter was Wessie's direct boss, Senior Superintendent Fred Blaaue, along with Sergeant Fryk Strydom of the Special Task Force. All of them had insights into ways to enhance Kontact, which I took on board and applied.

A couple of months after moving to Pretoria I travelled down to the Free State to run a two-week course for about sixty police instructors. The course was to be run in a soccer stadium in the heart of the local township. The stadium, built at the height of apartheid, was enormous, rising like an ocean liner out of a sea of tin shanties. It was redolent of the communist era of Eastern Europe, when dictators would build huge and enormously expensive cultural centres in the midst of squalor.

When I learnt that by seven in the morning the temperature would be in the mid-30s and by nine, 40°C, I decided to escape some of the heat by starting training at 3.45 am.

At 5.15 on the first morning, just as dawn was breaking, a group of men and women shuffled into the stadium and positioned themselves on one of the terraces. After ninety minutes of hard training I wondered if we were about to have an audience. One of the men told me this was the local gospel choir come to practise.

They began as the men and I turned back to our training. It was heart-lifting. It went beyond words and was as much a feeling as it was a sound, a low rumble of African harmonies. When they sang their traditional songs the voices were deep and hauntingly beautiful, and when they launched into some Christian hymns they brought a new and joyous sense of celebration and exuberance. It was a privilege to listen to them.

One song stayed with me for the rest of the day. It began with a mournful cry from a lone baritone, calling something that seemed as timeless as Africa itself. The cry went on for many heartbeats and then, suddenly, it stopped. What felt like an age passed and the silence seemed filled with expectation rather than nothingness. Another sound began, but so soft it was hard to tell if it really was a sound. Slowly a beat grew, one voice … then another. At some point, it was difficult to tell just when, there were many voices … a great many. Each was strong and proud and independent, yet each one was so obviously an indivisible part of those around it. Together the voices radiated power and dignity and purpose. I felt the skin on the back of my neck prickle and a sensation of unity echo around the shadows of the empty stands as the African sun blossomed over the horizon.

The choir came again on the following dawn, but on the third morning failed to show. I was disappointed and mentioned it to one of the senior officers on the course. He was surprised. 'I thought you wouldn't like all that noise and monkey chatter – I told the *kaffirs* to bugger off.'

That afternoon I went into the township looking for members of the choir and was pointed in the direction of a mountain of a man who was one of the singers. I told him it had been a mistake to send the choir away and that I wanted them to come back the following morning.

Which they did, and every day thereafter, and the amazing thing I noticed was how positively everyone on the course responded to the singing and to the atmosphere it generated. So much so that when the course finished there was a real bond among men who, themselves a microcosm of South Africa – Afrikaners, English-speaking white South Africans, Indians, Coloureds, Zulus and Xhosas – had all been deeply connected by Kontact and the haunting singing of the choir.

Back in Pretoria there was more good news. For months I'd been mainly training trainers, who had in turn gone out into the field as ambassadors of Kontact. They were good instructors and I was confident they had the professionalism not to cut corners when they trained their people. But, with the best will in the world, with the training at one remove I knew subtleties could be lost. It seemed someone else had worked that out too as, immediately on my return, I was told I'd be training Nelson Mandela's bodyguards directly.

For security reasons, the training had to be conducted within the grounds of the presidential estate, which made finding the right venue something of a challenge. I finally selected the lawn of the president's gardens as my training site. Sometimes, in the middle of training, I would see the gleaming presidential Mercedes sweep past in the sunshine on its way in or out of the estate.

One morning it stopped and I saw the rear window glide down; Nelson Mandela, Nobel Laureate and President of the Republic of South Africa, was watching me training his bodyguards. I couldn't help myself; as opposed as I was to show and exhibition I turned on the juice, putting the guys through their paces with a vengeance. Mandela watched for at least ten minutes, and I was hoping all the while that he was impressed.

When I glanced covertly at the limo I was shocked to see Mandela beckoning me over. I straightened up. 'Excuse me,' I said nonchalantly, 'the President wants me.' I swaggered towards the car and was about three metres away when Mandela jabbed a bony finger through the open window.

'You, Australian,' he said in that instantly recognisable voice, 'be careful of my flower beds.'

The Mercedes whispered away.

Hereford

The vision I'd had in the dawn of an Alice Springs car park had been realised to an extent far greater than I could possibly have hoped. Within two years of landing in Johannesburg, Kontact had become an officially accredited training program of the South African Police Service. People were booking months in advance to take part.

I had my small group of close friends, a nice place to live, even the occasional girlfriend – although nothing serious. I was also on respectful nodding terms with Nelson Mandela. I knew of course that in some circles there was jealousy; by South African standards I was being paid a small fortune to deliver my training, and a few disaffected people still referred to me as a *rooinek*. But with supporters like Wessie and Fred and Fryk endorsing Kontact, the jealousy was no more than an irritation.

It was a sign of how far my life had progressed that whereas in PNG I'd slept with a Smith & Wesson under my pillow, in Pretoria it was a notepad and pencil. Often I woke in the night to jot down a thought related to how I could improve my program – including the non-physical elements, such as negotiation and persuasive communication.

Having invested so much time and effort, I needed to be sure it was as good as I thought it was. I didn't want empty praise; I wanted honest and critical feedback from people whose opinion mattered, whose experience in operational unarmed combat spanned decades. For this, it was time to wash up on some new shore and start all over again.

Sitting in my flat I made a list of the world's top ten special forces units. These were internationally recognised units, trusted leaders with years of operational experience. One stood out above the others, Britain's 22 Special Air Service Regiment, the men who had so dramatically stormed the Iranian Embassy in London. I wanted them to judge my program.

I had an information pack printed and I posted it to the SAS base at Stirling Lines in Hereford in England. After a couple of months with no reply I mailed another. With still no response I was tempted to forget it. Life was good, yet something wouldn't let me rest.

The Japanese have a term for the idea of continuous improvement: *kaizen*. Put simply, *kaizen* is the reverse of complacency. It's a practical understanding that by consistently addressing small flaws and defects, large improvements will be achieved over time. On a number of levels Kontact embodied the spirit of *kaizen* – it was a vehicle that allowed me to challenge myself in ways I couldn't be challenged in a normal environment. There is nothing normal about the SAS. Books like

Bravo Two Zero introduced millions of readers to the world of British special forces, and I was one of the many intrigued by the exploits of authors like Steven Mitchell. The accounts he'd written as Andy McNab made me want to test myself in an arena that was professionally uncompromising. The prospect of teaching a training program of my own design to an organisation like the British SAS was as appealing as it was daunting.

After some persistence I obtained the phone number for Stirling Lines and dialled from my office in Pretoria. I was eventually put through to the unit's Second in Command. I introduced myself, saying I had an unarmed combat program I was sure the 2IC would find merit in. I'd scarcely launched into the benefits when the cold and chiselled voice at the other end told me it wasn't interested in anything I had to sell.

I responded by saying I appreciated his position, but I really believed he would see merit in the program if he saw how it worked. 'What about I call by your office, introduce myself, outline the program and perhaps we can arrange a demonstration date,' I said.

The voice, positively icy now, informed me that the regiment had an excellent unarmed combat program, one with which it was perfectly happy.

I repeated my offer of a meeting.

The voice cut like an Arctic wind. 'Are you deaf? Do I have a speech impediment?' The phone slammed down.

Opening my laptop, I tapped out a letter thanking the man for his time and saying, yet again, that I believed he would indeed see merit in my program. I finished by stating the date and time I'd call at his office. I faxed the letter, then went out and did something I'd never done before. I bought myself a business suit and an Italian silk tie. Back in my office I booked a ticket on the next available flight to Heathrow in London, grabbed my passport and caught a cab to the airport.

Less than thirty-six hours later, carrying a smart-looking buffalo-skin briefcase, I was marching through the main gate of Stirling Lines in Hereford. Doing my best to look like an officer and a gentleman I nodded curtly at the Ministry of Defence policeman at the gate. The policeman returned my nod and called me sir. I followed the path leading towards the barracks, reached a closed gate, and found my way blocked by another MoD cop. This one held a machine-gun across his chest and instead of nodding demanded to know what I wanted. I told him. The man jerked his head to indicate a booth to one side where another policeman sat behind glass which had the green sheen of bullet-proofing. This one asked for my ID, and I slid my business card under the glass. The man read it aloud, slowly, before asking, his tone dripping with condescension, 'And what do you want to know, son?'

'Nothing from you, thanks. I'm here to see the Second in Command.'

The cop gave me the hard eye, grunted and pressed a buzzer and a wire-mesh security gate swung open. Walking through, I found myself across the counter from the man, now murmuring into the phone. 'Yes, sir. Certainly, sir.' The cop put down the phone and, without a word, left the booth.

Afterwards, I was never sure if I waited an hour or just five minutes before a fit-looking trooper wearing the unit's coveted sandy beret and winged-dagger badge marched in and motioned me to follow him. Even at the double it took a while through a succession of corridors, walkways and across frost-covered playing fields to reach the Second in Command's office.

The first thing I noticed was my fax on the desk. The second thing was the man's face, about as welcoming as a gun turret. He waved me peremptorily to a wooden seat and told me to get on with it. I was ten minutes into my presentation before the face behind the desk showed the slightest sign of animation, but after fifteen minutes he was asking questions, and inside half an hour he'd agreed to a full demonstration.

I walked out of the barracks as if I was walking on air.

A week later I was back. In the barracks' gymnasium I faced twenty of the regiment's finest, their body language shouting at me, 'We are the best in the world and who the hell are you?'

I knew I wasn't going to get a second chance with

this audience. If I was going to make this work, I had to go for broke. Turning to the Second in Command I said, 'I need a volunteer. The best you've got.' After some murmuring among the group a large man strolled out to the front. I looked at him. 'I'm going to give you thirty seconds to take me to the ground and make me submit. If you can get a wristlock on me, do it. If you can dislocate my shoulder, go for it. If you can apply some type of secret ninja special forces choke hold and knock me out, don't hold back. Whatever you do, do it with *absolute commitment*. Okay?'

The big trooper dropped his chin and raised his eyebrows in that universal nuance of body language that states, unequivocally, 'Yeah, not a problem. You're a moron and this is too easy.'

Then I put on a blindfold.

I raised my hand to signal the trooper when to attack. I felt confident, even though I knew how easy it was for something to go wrong.

I dropped my hand.

The big trooper charged in like a bull. After fifteen seconds both the blindfold and a chunk of my hair had been ripped off. But the trooper hadn't forced me to submit. Keeping my eyes closed I knelt down and waited for the trooper to attack again. He came in even harder. Fifteen seconds later the 2IC called time and I opened my eyes. The trooper, breathing hard, gave me a lopsided grin and ruffled what was left of my hair. I'd won, but there was nothing magical about what had taken place. All I'd done was employ one of the most uncomplicated forms of defence that exists: noncompliance. When the trooper pushed, I pulled. When he grabbed high, I grabbed low. When he used linear force, I used circular evasion. My counters were not 'techniques' as such, rather spontaneous movement intended to frustrate and neutralise the trooper's efforts. And it worked.

The 2IC strode with purpose across the gym floor. 'Let's work out a date. You'll have the price you quoted.'

To show my gratitude for all he'd done for me, I flew Albertus Wessels in from South Africa to help run the course at Stirling Lines. Wessie had become an instructor in the program and the South African Police, delighted that one of their own would be training 22 SASR, sent him to Hereford on paid leave. Afterwards, when it was all over, Wessie moaned, 'If this is your idea of thanking me, I'd prefer you were an ungrateful *rooinek*.' He was only half joking. As the course instructors, it was our responsibility to set the pace in accordance with the collective ability of the group, while always applying a fraction more effort than any individual student.

The course was exhausting; six days of intense free-motion drills with such a massive build-up of lactic acid that, by the end of the first day, my body was screaming. I staggered back to the mess, fell on my bed and stayed there, too exhausted to eat, until the following morning. At the end of day three I seriously wondered if I'd have the strength to continue and, on the evening of the final day, I was so tired and sore it even hurt to brush my teeth.

Now I understood. Not for nothing were these men considered the best by so many in the jungle of special forces. Their fitness and their attitude were almost unbelievable. On the first day, having introduced a basic knife defence exercise – a dynamic, free-flowing activity using a marker pen – one of the troopers had his eyelid ripped open. With one hand held across his eye, the guy casually jogged over to the base's medical centre, had it stitched, and then rejoined the class – as if nothing out of the ordinary had taken place.

Of all the Kontact courses Wessie and I presented together this one was by far the most challenging. We knew that every word we said, every move we made, was being critically evaluated. We had to deliver rock-solid, practical value. And that's what we did – well, that's what we aimed to do, but part of the challenge was that the participants were all so incredibly difficult to read. It was like each one of them was a professional poker player. Their body language gave no indication of what they were thinking and when they asked a question their tone was infuriatingly hard to interpret.

When the course was over, I knew I couldn't have done any better but I was still unsure about how the participants had viewed it. Usually, when a course ends students move around the class, shaking hands with each other and with the presenters, and have a bit of a joke. In most cases, someone in the group will get up and say a few words of thanks. Not this time. After my final comments, everyone just picked up their course study notes and walked out of the gym. Only one person came across to shake my hand. He didn't actually say anything, he just looked at me, gave a slight nod and then walked off – leaving me none-the-wiser as to how my program had been received.

I found out ten days later, back in South Africa. Still bruised and battered from the training at Hereford, I was catching up on some paperwork in my office in Pretoria – the same office where I'd first phoned the 2IC and been told, in no uncertain terms, that he was not in the slightest bit interested in my training program. After the fax machine on my desk started to print, I was hit with an equal mix of anticipation and dread when I saw where the message was being sent from: Hereford.

I almost reached out to turn off the machine. A part of me couldn't bear the thought of having my program slammed. I wouldn't care if the person slamming it was a suburban armchair expert, or a Constable Plod who'd never been anywhere or done anything, but the men at Stirling Lines were nothing like that. There was no escaping the hard fact that their opinion mattered. So, I didn't turn off the fax. Instead, I waited with bated breath as the single A4 sheet of paper slowly, painstakingly, inched out.

22 FEB '96 8:58 FROM COMMCEN-HEREFORD PAGE.001

F Sigs 927
(Int.9/92)

Caveat O/C
Covering

Facsimile Transmission Cover Sheet

Transmission Details			Document Details	
Serial Number:	Date and Time of Transmission:		Reference:	
From: TPS HEREFORD	Fax Number: 01432 35[redacted]		Subject: KONTAKT TRG	
To: MR R REDENBACH	Fax Number: 0027 12[redacted]			
			Total number of pages including this cover sheet	1

Authorizing Officer	Transmit Operators
Rank, Name and Appointment: [redacted]	Rank/Grade and Name:
Signature: [redacted]	Signature:

Message/Remarks:

HQ Hereford Garrison
Stirling Lines
Hereford HR2 6HF

Rob,

Thanks for the reports on the Kontakt course students. The course was very well received by all, especially the more senior members (who can be quite cynical of new techniques – but not this time!). I am interested in running a 5 day course, similar to that just gone, before the end March or latest v. early April 96. I am not sure of numbers – short lead time accepted!

PS Pse note address top right.

Covering
Caveat O/C
Classification

Hand-written by the 2IC, the message included: *The course was very well received by all, especially the more senior members (who can be quite cynical of new techniques – but not this time!).* Beyond that, they wanted another course – which is the best feedback.

My next trip to Hereford was supposed to be for five days – it ended up being four months. Despite my antipodean origins, I was signed on to the books of the SAS reserve unit, 'L' Detachment, which meant I could live on base, eat in the mess and wear a British army uniform, except for the coveted SAS beret and badge. I even had a British army serial number. In my time with the regiment, I provided training for the officers and men, as well as training with them. This included weapons training at Catterick in North Yorkshire, and travelling with the regiment to Wales, to their training ground in the stark, dark, hauntingly beautiful Brecon Beacons. I trained, shot, ate and drank with these men who were as different from the Hollywood stereotype of special forces as Hereford rain is different from Pretorian sunshine.

Of the many rewards I gained from my time at Hereford, a stand out was learning that the SAS have their own version of *kaizen*: inscribed on the memorial clock tower at Stirling Lines is a poem by James Elroy Flecker;

But who are ye in rags and rotten shoes,
You dirty bearded, blocking up the way?

We are the Pilgrims, master; we shall go
Always a little further; it may be
Beyond that last blue mountain barred with snow
Across that angry or that glimmering sea.

As one veteran expressed to me; he loved the concept of 'a little further' and used it as something of a mantra – the idea that if you keep putting one foot in front of the other towards your goal, if you keep making imperceptible improvements with every workout you do, or speech you give, or picture you draw, that you can edge towards getting halfway decent at anything you choose. It's a powerful concept.

I couldn't agree more.

During my time with the regiment I continued to refine Kontact, and thanks to the company I was keeping my focus broadened as I started to absorb the leadership views of the people around me. Whether it was delivering Kontact training at Stirling Lines, 'tabbing' Pen-y-Fan or having a pint or three of Guinness at Saxty's Bar in Hereford, there were priceless opportunities to tap into the wisdom of others. The best example I had exposure to came from Andy Chalmers, the 2IC.

Not a man to suffer fools, Chalmers (not his real name) explained, 'We've been on continuous operations since 1945 and because of this we are very aware of the need to lead well. My own ethos is that officers exist because of their men.

'There must be a connection, understanding and

sympathy with the soldier's job, however, officers must gain respect and not lean too far towards their men – this was the advice of a sergeant and close comrade of mine when I was a troop commander. With that respect comes the soldier's understanding of tough decisions delivered by a leader who genuinely cares. In special forces the divide between officer and men is greatly reduced, but the respect and expectation remain.'

Chalmers' ethos saw him go on to have a stellar career, which included commanding a multinational force of 2000 operators in Afghanistan in 2011. What I particularly liked about Chalmers was that he was prepared to accept personal risk if it had the potential to help the people he led. In the two decades I've now known him, I've observed that some managers, in contrast to genuine leaders, are far more concerned about feathering their own nest than making a positive, long-term difference. In Chalmers' case it would have been safer not to hire me. I was an unknown quantity. He didn't need to break from the status quo. However, he is one of those outstanding decision-makers who is prepared to try something different with the goal of continually seeking improvement.

***

It was easy to enjoy living in England. I was absolutely loving my work. I had some good friends, including Andy Chalmers, and with most weekends spent in London's West End, life was purposeful and fun. Andy invited me to 'have a crack' at joining the regiment and becoming a badged member. I was tempted to try for it, but I knew it was never going to happen. Running, marching and carrying extreme loads is the bread and butter of a special forces soldier. While I could swim, cycle and teach Kontact with my damaged knee, even a light jog would leave me limping for a week. There was no way I would pass selection.

So I returned to Pretoria and focused once more on developing Kontact, analysing feedback and conducting evaluation seminars for the police who had been presenting training in my absence under the supervision of Wessie. It was a hectic time, with months of back-to-back courses across the country. I was working hard, as were my assistant instructors. To reward them I arranged a special night, hiring the gallery of wildlife artist Martin Koch, where I had a team of caterers transform the space into an elegant private restaurant.

It was a wonderful evening, and after the meal I gave my first ever after-dinner speech, thanking every individual in turn for their help in making Kontact so successful, saving for last Wessie, the man who, above all others, had given me my start.

I concluded with, 'The last time I said thank you to Wessie he called me a *rooinek* and said he'd prefer it if I never did it again. Well, I'm sorry Wessie, but —'

I had commissioned an original Martin Koch oil painting of a lion, which was hanging on the

Top: A partner resistance exercise – one small part of a much larger jigsaw I would christen Kontact. Lae, Papua New Guinea. 1992.

Right: Buffalo hunting, Morobe Province, Papua New Guinea. 1993.

Below: The first Kontact course, Pietersburg, Transvaal. Wessie is on my left. South Africa. 1994.

Top: Kontact training on top of Table Mountain, Cape Town. 1996.

Middle: At the SAS clock tower, Stirling Lines, Hereford. I'm in the back row, on the right. My friend and former Hong Kong kickboxing champion, Seb, is in the 3rd row, second from the left. 1996.

Right: On leave from 'L' Detachment, 22 SASR. Tragically, within a year of this photo being taken Seb would be killed – not in combat, but by a drunk driver in London. 1996.

Top: Members of the Los Angeles FBI Special Weapons and Tactics team take part in Kontact training. California. 1997. **(Photo courtesy of US National Tactical Officers Association.)**

Bottom Left: From first date to wedding in twelve days. 1997.

Bottom Right: The first attempt at this photo failed. The camera didn't work. Thankfully the President said "Don't worry, Aussie. Come back tomorrow with a new camera and we'll try again." 1997.

Top: The President holding our son, Liam. 1998.

Middle: SOCOG's one-armed unarmed combat instructor, 1 Commando base, Randwick. 1999.

Below: Corporate team-building at my old Battalion, Holsworthy. NSW. 2001.

Top: After moving from Soldiers Point to the Gold Coast. 2002.

Middle: Bronte's 3rd birthday (she's the one with the cool sunglasses). 2003.

Below: Presenting personal safety training to field staff from UNICEF and World Vision. Nairobi, Kenya. 2005.

Top: A lucky escape. It doesn't get much closer than the bullet hole in the top right-hand section. Baghdad, Iraq. 2005.

Left: Standard kit for Baghdad's Red Zone. Iraq. 2005.

Below: After appearing on *Sunrise* for the first time, one viewer sent an email that said "Nice work. You were factual, realistic and the voice of reason. I assume we will never see you on TV again." 2007.

Top: Still dazed, a few minutes after our LandCruiser hit a pot hole and rolled. Kabul, Afghanistan. 2008.

Right: Aid work, Nangarhar Province, Afghanistan. 2008.

Below: Speaking at the Global Leadership Summit in Singapore – the largest gathering of CEOs in the world at that time. 2012.

Top: Following Stephen Covey's advice and Sharpening the Saw. Gold Coast. 2014

Middle: Signing books after my 500th corporate keynote. Sheraton Grand Mirage Resort. 2016.

Below: Recording *Poetry For Men (who thought they'd never like poetry)*. 2020.

nearby wall. I lifted it down. 'Wessie, this is a token of my appreciation for the risk you took in putting your trust in my program, and me. Thanks.'

I think I detected tears in Wessie's eyes; I was feeling a bit emotional myself. This celebration was the culmination of years of hard work.

A week later I received a request from the Honolulu Police Department, offering me an all-expenses-paid trip to Hawaii to train instructors at their police academy. It put a smile on my face: for the first time I was washing ashore at someone else's request and expense.

One of the participants on the HPD course was Boisse Correa – who would go on to become Chief of Police. Boisse was a pleasure to work with; skilled, smart and highly respected. In part, thanks to his positive evaluation of Kontact, my work in Hawaii brought me to the attention of the US Federal Bureau of Investigation, who requested I fly to Los Angeles to conduct a basic course for the Bureau's SWAT team there. And so I met Doug Kane, the team commander, another outstanding leader of the same ilk as Wessie and Chalmers. After the basic course, Doug wrote a detailed article about Kontact in the Fall 1997 edition of *The Tactical Edge*, the official journal of the US National Tactical Officers Association. Doug also requested an advanced Kontact program, and it was in the course of this that I ended up going on drug raids with his team.

Johannesburg

I'd been away for over a month, first in Los Angeles with Doug Kane's team, then back in London running another course for Andy Chalmers, this time at Chelsea Barracks. I hadn't seen any of my friends for a while, so I called them when I got back to Johannesburg and suggested we have lunch at a restaurant in Sandton.

It was good to be back in South Africa: the weather was perfect; Wessie, Fred and Fryk were good company as always, and we were celebrating with a few bottles of wine and a lot of laughter. But glancing around the busy, noisy restaurant I suddenly lost interest in my food.

'What's got into you?' Fred asked.

'That woman over there. She's gorgeous.'

The others eyeballed her. 'Yeah, she's not bad.'

'I'm going over to talk to her. See if I can get a date.'

They laughed. 'Forget it, man. What would a creature like that see in a *moffie* like you? She's going to tell you to *voetsek*.'

Ignoring them, I stood up and threaded my way through the crowded tables to where the woman was having lunch with a couple of girlfriends. I introduced myself, then added, 'but you can call me Red.'

'Red? Why?'

'It's a long story, but I'll be happy to tell you it over dinner one evening. If you give me your number I'll call you.'

She smiled and said nothing, considering me with clear, cool eyes.

'So, what's your name?' I asked.

'Natasha.'

'Really? Do you know, that's my favourite name.'

She laughed, a deep, throaty chuckle. 'You'll have to do better than that.'

'It's true.'

'Even if it is, I'm not giving you my phone number. I only give that to my friends.'

'Well, I'm a friendly guy.'

'I'm sure you are, Red,' she said levelly, 'but so is my neighbourhood dogcatcher. Doesn't mean to say I'll be giving him my phone number.'

I could see she was someone who knew her own mind and to push for her number wouldn't get me anywhere worthwhile. I wondered if I'd made a connection though; she had used my name and there was something in her eyes that told me she might, perhaps, be a little intrigued.

'Okay, then let me give you *my* number.' I slipped a business card from my pocket.

She took it reluctantly. 'Why would I want your number? It's not as if I'm going to call you.'

'Well, you never know. You could change your mind and decide that I would be a good guy to go out with; that you'd actually enjoy having dinner with me.'

She shook her head. 'Don't hold your breath, Red.'

I returned to the table where the others were waiting to grill me.

'So, did you get a date?'

'No.'

They laughed. 'What about her phone number? Did you get that?'

'No. But I gave her mine.'

They laughed louder. 'Did she tell you to *voetsek*?' I knew they were pulling my leg, but what they didn't appreciate was that, even in the few seconds I'd stood at her table, something about Natasha had got to me. I tried to change the subject. 'Okay, time to admit something: I've picked up some of your heathen language, but what's this *voetsek*?'

'It's a word you use when some annoying little dog starts snapping at your ankles,' Fryk announced.

'Or when an irritating Aussie interrupts your lunch,' Wessie chuckled.

I laughed too. These guys were good friends, but, like mates everywhere, when it came to women they were bound to give the single guy, me, a hard time. It was a natural law of the universe.

I glanced across at Natasha's table and caught her looking at me. She looked away quickly.

She stayed in my mind.

Over the following weeks I went back to the restaurant in Sandton a few times in the hope she might be there. She never was, and my disappointment was much sharper than it had any right to be. Why should I care so much? I had only spoken to her for a minute. But it looked like I'd have to live with it. She wasn't going to call me.

***

I travelled north, accompanying Fred and Derrick – another senior SAPS officer – on a semi-official South African Police Service tour of goodwill to Zambia, Zimbabwe and Botswana. We cruised down the Chobe River by ferry, watching elephants grazing majestically in the distance, giraffes feeding on acacias, and crocodiles concealed in nearby mud flats. At the end of a long day, we set up camp in the Savuti Marshes. Feeling a little stiff after unpacking our gear from the four-wheel drive, I decided to stretch my legs. Fred and Derrick were happy to stay in camp and prepare the evening meal while I went for a walk along the riverbank.

I'd gone about two kilometres when I caught a flash of movement away to my left. Whatever it was, it was reasonably large, brownish in colour, and fast. Knowing it was probably stupid to keep going, I kept going. About fifty metres on I caught another flash of movement, this time to my right, and closer. I scanned the area and was just starting to hope I was imagining things when, looking straight ahead, what I saw made my legs go rigid. Sitting in the middle of the track, staring intently and directly at me, was a large baboon. It was less than twenty metres away. Maybe it was just being territorial, but I had never seen such molten hostility and blatant contempt pouring from a set of eyes. I could actually *feel* the ape's aggression, as if it were a physical weapon.

To my left, I caught another glimpse of movement. To my right, yet another flash of fur and limbs. I quickly glanced over my shoulder; four more baboons were circling behind me.

The fear I felt at that point was, simply, primordial. My throat contracted, my heart rate spiked, my legs shook, and I started to sweat; not the healthy sweat that comes from a good workout, but a sickening, cold sweat that consumes and inhibits.

The baboon blocking the path was clearly the troop leader. Not only did he have an overwhelming air of regal arrogance, but the other baboons – of which the number seemed to be growing by the second – were clearly deferring to him with head bobs and furtive glances. It was as if they were minions humbly requesting his royal consent to rip me to pieces.

Fear riveted me to the ground.

I could hear the blood thumping in my temples.

Motionless, the baboon stared.

And stared.

What seemed to be an eternity slowly ticked by.

And still the baboon stared.

Suddenly, the creature burst into action; in a single bound it sprang forward, bared its teeth and *yelled* … it did not growl, or howl or make a noise you would expect from an animal; it *yelled*.

I have no idea what prompted me to do what

I did next; it did not conform to the Kontact principle of *not* matching your opponent's mode of attack (don't box a boxer, don't wrestle a wrestler, and so on), but it did demonstrate noncompliance and refusing to submit easily. I too sprang forward, bared my teeth and yelled at the top of my lungs.

The effect was instantaneous; the baboon's eyes widened in shock – I was now close enough to see his eyes clearly – and he seemed to stop in mid-air.

I yelled again.

Reluctantly, and with a look of hatred that remained palpable, the baboon withdrew a few paces. I yelled again as I retreated away from the baboon and back towards the camp.

Every few paces I had to stop, bare my teeth and growl at the closest baboon. They followed me for at least half an hour, which seemed more like half a day.

When I arrived back at camp, Derrick – lounging on a canvas chair, with a beer in one hand and a novel in the other – casually remarked, 'You took your time. Another couple of beers and I was going to start thinking about seeing if you were okay.'

***

When I got back to my flat in Pretoria the little red dot on my answering machine was flashing like a strobe light. It was late and I was half tempted to leave the messages until morning, but I grabbed a pad and ballpoint and sat by the machine.

Natasha's call came halfway through the sequence. I recognised her voice instantly. She had left a number. I glanced at my watch. Damn … damn … too late to call her now. I went to bed feeling as if I'd won the lottery, and I called her the following morning.

She sounded a little reticent, but said she'd decided she might have dinner with me, although only if she chose where and when. She wasn't used to dating, she said, which surprised me. I'd have thought someone as beautiful as she would have been fighting admirers off with a flamethrower.

Her choice of restaurant was unpretentious, with good food and friendly staff. We talked easily. She'd had her share of tragedy: though young, Natasha was a widow. Kevin, her husband, had been killed in a car accident when she was six weeks pregnant with their second child, Cuan. It had taken her almost five years to recover, but now, she told me across the candlelight, she was emerging, getting ready to face life once more.

By the end of the evening I knew I was in love. Really in love.

Twelve days later we were married.

In a simple, flower-strewn ceremony at which Wessie was best man, I was adopted by Natasha and her children, Reilly and Cuan.

A few days after our honeymoon, as I was finishing a training session on the presidential lawns, I noticed an aide hovering close to the beloved flowerbeds. Grabbing a towel I jogged across the lawn.

'Is it true you have recently married a South African woman?' the aide asked.

'Yes. Why, is that a problem?'

The aide shook his head. 'No. The President wishes to congratulate you. He asks if you and your wife would have lunch with him at Government House. Next Friday?'

Our names were announced as we were ushered into a large dining room where we were surprised to find ourselves the only guests. As the double doors closed silently behind us, Mandela stood up, his eyes on Natasha.

'Natasha,' he said in his gravelly voice, 'you are truly beautiful. Tell me, why did you marry *him*?' The light-hearted remark set the tone for a relaxed and thoroughly enjoyable experience.

Close up, I saw that I was about the same height and build as Mandela, who told us that in his youth he had been a serious distance runner and boxer. The science and strategy of boxing, he said, intrigued him, while cross-country running had taught him the valuable lesson that training counted for far more than natural ability. That discovery – that diligence and effort could compensate for a lack of natural talent – had stood him in good stead in everything he had done since. He had seen countless young people with outstanding natural ability who had not had the self discipline to maximise their advantages. That really struck a chord with me.

When the time came for us to leave, I said, 'Thank you, sir. It's been a privilege.'

He placed a hand on my shoulder and said, 'I prefer not to be called sir, especially by my guests. Why don't you call me Madiba?'

Walking away I reflected on how often I'd been forced to address some snobby subaltern or pissed punter as sir. It seemed ironic that the one person I'd met in my entire life who I'd have been happy to call sir should refuse it. It was a lesson that true greatness comes quietly and with humility.

***

Natasha fell pregnant almost immediately and we moved into a big house complete with a swimming pool and separate maid's quarters, hiring both a maid and a gardener to take care of the domestic chores.

It was, without doubt, the good life. My business was now firmly embedded in a score of South African agencies, and although I still made excursions away to run courses, in my newfound domesticity I limited my overseas trips. For a range of reasons I didn't like being away from Tash and the children; most critically because of security concerns.

Although South Africa had been very good to me, it was, undeniably, a violent country. Carjacking, home invasion, murder and rape were all common. Within a few kilometres of our house, five men, armed with AK47s, had broken into a home and, in the process of robbing the place, shot and killed the mother and father of an eleven-year-old girl who they then proceeded to rape on the floor beside her dead parents. The incident was considered too commonplace to make the national news.

The violence that previously had been a peripheral concern to me now loomed central to my life. I was a married man with a wife and the responsibility of young children, a responsibility that hugely increased with the birth of our son, Liam.

So much of our life was concentrated on security. Despite the ever-present risk of carjacking I drove the children to school through fifty-five minutes of rush-hour traffic rather than send them on a school bus that had been hijacked by men with machine-guns three times in three months. Coming home every evening, Tash and I followed a ritual that would have seemed laughably neurotic if it hadn't been so necessary.

And so deadly serious.

Driving into our street I'd check the footpath, fence line and gates for anything unusual while listening for our dobermans to start barking, thereby confirming they were still alive. Arriving in front of the eight-foot gates I'd check the rear and side mirrors for anyone behind the car before leaping out, locking the car door and opening the gates while Tash climbed over the central console and put the car into reverse, ready for a quick getaway. All being normal I'd open the gates to allow Tash to drive in quickly before I slammed them shut. I hated the whole ritual, especially as Tash, pregnant with our second child, found it increasingly difficult to climb around in the car.

Like many South Africans we were living like mediaeval barons walled up in our castle, afraid to venture out into a world filled with danger. Our home was a cage; gilded on the inside, ugly on the outside with high fences and gates; every window barred. What was worse, whole sections of the population were descending into a sea of hysteria over personal security. People were paranoid and trigger-happy, primed to erupt at the least provocation.

Returning to my car in a car park at our local shopping centre one day, I watched a guy zoom into a bay that a woman, waiting in her car, had been indicating her rights to. It was the kind of bullying behaviour I had no time for, made worse by the fact that the guy and his passenger were openly laughing at their cleverness. Without thinking, I went up to their car and tapped on the window. The man burst out of his vehicle like a tornado, crashing his door open and slamming me backwards before bulldozing me against the side of the next car with his heavy gut. The man was big and had a long reach. He threw a punch, which I half jammed and half evaded before driving my elbow into his head. He went down.

The woman driver seemed both grateful and impressed, saying repeatedly, 'No-one wants to get involved or help other people any more.' Within minutes the police arrived and I was arrested for assault, and some days later I received a writ from the guy I'd dropped, suing me for damages for the sum of a million rand. In the end the charges were dropped and the claim for damages came to nothing. I considered myself lucky, because the woman's solicitor had written to me telling me that his client did not wish to be involved and especially did not want to be called as a witness in any court proceedings.

It gave me something to think about. Many South Africans were permanently armed. Supposing the guy had had a gun in the car? I was a husband and a father who had risked himself – for what? For the sake of decent behaviour and a woman whose commitment and integrity went no deeper than her make-up.

I talked about my concerns with Tash.

'I want us to live in a place where kids can walk down the street to buy an ice cream without the very good chance of being murdered or raped,' I said. 'Last year, this country had more than *seventeen thousand* recorded murders. Australia, with half the population, had three hundred.'

She wasn't enthusiastic. She was a seventh-generation South African, her family part of the country's fabric. To go to Australia would be dragging the older children up by the roots, taking them away from close-knit families that had seen them through the death of their father. And Australia would cost. While we were reasonably affluent in the Republic, with the exchange rate and the comparative price of property, resettling in Australia would mean starting over again.

But things were changing. Mandela was coming to the end of a political term and had announced he would not run again for President. I had a notion that when he stepped down life might be different, and not in a good way.

And then, as if on cue, Andy Chalmers called me from Stirling Lines at Hereford. He had a contact, an Australian SAS major, who was one of the senior security managers for the 2000 Sydney Olympic Games. The Olympic committee wanted me to teach Kontact to Australian police and military instructors assigned to Dignitary and Athlete Protection. It was a big, prestigious contract. And very tempting.

What finally settled matters was being woken one night to the sound of screaming. The screams were coming from out on the street, from what sounded like a woman in fear for her life. I leapt out of bed and rushed towards the front of the house, checking on the children as I went. The woman's screams had woken them, and as I scuttled from room to room they too began screaming. Reaching a front window I peered into the ethereal glow of the streetlights to see a hysterical woman running the length of the street. Racing after her was a man, bellowing abuse and waving a piece of timber longer than his arm.

My instinct was to rush outside, scale the gates and deck the guy. But I stopped myself. Was it a set-up? A classic ruse to lure me out of the house so men with AK47s could get in, murder Tash and rape the children? But supposing the woman was an innocent victim? I could help. But should I? I had a family. Surely, they had to come first. I wanted to help the woman but … I moved from foot to foot, torn one way then the other.

Finally I realised that in my immobility I had already decided. I turned back to the window to watch the man and woman disappear into the gloom at the far end of the street. It was the right decision, I told myself, the only decision; I was a husband and father. I couldn't take unnecessary risks.

But, if it was the right decision – why did it feel so wrong?

It was a terrible feeling, and I had an idea that if I stayed in South Africa it was one I'd experience again.

Together, Tash and I made the decision to leave. In Australia we would stop living behind high walls and barred windows. In Australia we could raise our children without the ever-present threat of violence. Australia was a land of opportunity. It was the lucky country. And if I could be successful in South Africa … then surely I could be in my homeland. Already, thanks to Andy Chalmers, I had a lucrative contract lined up. It was definitely the right thing to do.

We were invited to the presidential estate to say goodbye and I got one of the bodyguards to take a photograph of us: Madiba, grinning and holding Liam in his arms, Natasha, the older children and me.

Madiba noticed Natasha was pregnant again and talked about children and family life. 'You must remember, Aussie,' he said, 'there is only one thing a child owes its parent.'

'What's that, Madiba?'

'Nothing. A child does not owe a parent respect. A child does not owe a parent gratitude. These are gifts the child *chooses* to give. But only if the parent deserves them.'

There were many things I was going to miss about South Africa: Nelson Mandela was definitely one of them.

Soldiers Point

By South African standards we'd lived extremely well. All that changed when we arrived in Australia. The rand to dollar exchange rate took the wind right out of our financial sails, and for twice the amount we'd been paying in Johannesburg, we rented a small three-bedroom unit that was a shock to the system. It was, however, safe and close to the water in a pretty area called Soldiers Point, near Newcastle.

We were marking time until the Olympics contract came on line. Greg Shaw, the Australian SAS major who was a senior security manager for the Games, was supportive, but the whole issue of Olympics security was beset by politics and vested interests. I lost count of the number of times I travelled to Sydney on my own money to be told, yet again, that the start date had been postponed; the extent of the training, and associated budget, reduced.

In the meantime I needed to develop Kontact in Australia.

This was easier said than done.

I had new brochures printed outlining my program and sent copies off to state and federal police authorities, the military and other target groups.

Their response reminded me of my early days in South Africa, with the added twist that not only was there a lack of interest in what I was offering, but also a weird kind of jealousy and disbelief. And though I supplied contact details for Fred Blaaue, Doug Kane and Andy Chalmers, not one person I approached in Australia contacted these people to verify my claims.

I needed something to kick-start my business.

'I think I'm going to write a book,' I said to Natasha. I had just finished my nightly ritual of reading to the children and had returned to the lounge carrying the kids' copy of *The Power of One*.

Natasha, feeding our newest son, Blake, looked up. 'What about?'

'A book about some of the concepts I've been refining over the past few years. Partly about self-defence, but mostly about attitude and outlook – I'm going to call it *Perform With Confidence*.'

'That's a great idea. You write very well.'

Tash's response surprised me, in a pleasant way. I don't know why, but I'd expected some resistance to the idea, even a dismissal. During my years of teaching English in Asia I'd put a lot of time and energy into tailoring lesson notes for my students. That experience had improved my ability to write, but I still wondered if I could produce a book worth reading. Given the book's title, the irony of my self doubt wasn't lost on me and I decided the best way forward was to just start. So I did.

Even so it took a lot of effort to write a book, and hard as it was to write it, it was even harder to sell. I approached over a dozen publishers with my manuscript. Most took months to respond with a terse, dismissive two-line rejection; some wrote a few extra lines to tell me there was no demand for a book like mine. Some didn't reply at all. Yet the more I was rejected the more determined I was to see it in bookshops. There seemed to be only one option.

'We'll have to publish it ourselves,' I told Tash.

'That sounds expensive.'

'It is. But a publisher is just a middleman; they cover printing and distribution, but their share of the proceeds is four times as much as the author. So why use a publisher? In the end this book will make money.'

'And in the meantime?'

'In the meantime, we use our savings to cover the cost of printing.'

'You mean the money that's our deposit for a home?'

'Yep.'

Together we managed the project of publishing the book; we were the editors, the typesetters, the proofreaders, the graphic designers. We chose the paper, selected the printer and began marketing the book, selling it direct to bookshops in Queensland and New South Wales.

My fledgling attempt at writing press releases got me some slots on local and national radio stations talking about my book and the work I'd done overseas.

Attention from the radio stations triggered interest from the *Today Show*, which filmed me running a Kontact course in Sydney at the University of NSW. The exposure not only helped sales of the book, but also aroused the interest of the prime-time *60 Minutes*. The program, which had been looking at security aspects of the Olympics for months, wanted to investigate how Kontact fitted into the overall security of the Sydney Olympics.

I was delighted, and I enjoyed the irony. After more than twelve months since being approached for the job, I was still waiting for the committee of SOCOG to give me the green light to start my training. Now, still without a firm start date, Kontact was becoming the focus of media attention.

Not being a political animal I didn't appreciate the position I was in. Since I wasn't yet contracted to SOCOG, I was a free agent and therefore at liberty to talk about security training at the Olympics. Somebody on the inside realised this and suddenly there were urgent moves to sign me up, the unseemly haste flushing out the hidden bias that had been holding the contract back. When it was reported that I was about to be signed, a middle manager with the New South Wales police fell out of his tree, firing off an email where he demanded to know, 'Who is this goon? I've never heard of him. What is Kontact anyway? Can't this idiot even spell?'

Yet despite middle-ranking policemen throwing their toys out of the cot, I was finally signed to provide training for the Sydney Olympics to instructors from the Federal Police, the Australian SAS, the State Protection Group and the New South Wales police. The contract specifically prohibited the media from filming the training, which killed the option of a *60 Minutes* story, but I didn't care. My primary interest was teaching, not television.

A couple of days before the course was due to start at 1 Commando base in Randwick, I received a call from a producer of *A Current Affair*. He'd seen the *Today Show* story and was interested in filming my training. I explained that I couldn't talk about the Olympics.

'Yeah, yeah, that's okay mate,' the producer said. 'I want to do a story on *you*. I think you've got potential. Your self-defence stuff might make a good three or four-minute story. Get you to do a few fancy moves.'

'What do you mean by fancy moves?' I asked.

'You know, a bit of Bruce Lee and Jackie Chan. Smash some bricks. That kind of thing. You can do that, can't you?'

'I've never been attacked by a brick, so why would I hit one?'

There was a moment's silence.

'Look, mate, I don't think you understand *television*. You've got to impress the viewers. Make them go wow, mate.'

I was getting irritated with this stranger who called me mate. 'Look, I don't do martial arts training. I provide honest and realistic unarmed combat training. It's supposed to *do* good, not *look* good.'

'Yeah, but you've still got to put on a show, mate.'

'I think you've got the wrong stooge, *mate*.' I put the phone down.

Straight away I wondered if I'd done the right thing. The old saying 'any publicity is good publicity' sprang to mind. But to have given the producer what he wanted would have been a sell-out. It would have been a slap in the face to people like Wessie who had helped me so much. A good PR boost would have been a fine thing, but I couldn't let that be a priority. Forget it, I told myself. I had more important things to focus on.

If I had been a fatalist I would have sworn the SOCOG contract was cursed from the start. On the afternoon of the first day I was wrestling with a guy from the SAS when my bad knee gave way and I fell awkwardly. To avoid landing on my knee, I twisted in mid-air and hit the ground elbow first. The angle was all wrong and my full body weight forced the top of my right humerus out of my shoulder joint.

Lying on the grass staring up at the sky I focused on my breathing, forcing the part of my mind screaming at the pain to concentrate on the slow, rhythmic supply of oxygen. Of course my breathing didn't make the pain go away, but it did help. Slightly.

At the Emergency Department of the Prince of Wales Hospital, just down the road from the commando base, X-rays confirmed what was excruciatingly obvious; my arm was fractured, my shoulder dislocated. The duty doctor also predicted possible nerve damage.

The next morning, with my shoulder heavily taped and my arm in a padded sling, I was back at the commando base where the guys made a lot of jokes about one-armed unarmed combat instructors. I laughed with them – I could see the funny side, although the nature of Kontact made it difficult to teach effectively with one arm in a sling. Fortunately I was being assisted by my friend Graham Kuerschner, a forty-year veteran of martial science; with his help the course went well and feedback was positive.

The opinion of the medical specialists in Newcastle was anything but positive. My shoulder was permanently damaged they told me. It was not good news, especially as Natasha was pregnant again. Soon I would have six other mouths to feed while my profession, my primary source of income, was under threat of going down the toilet.

'What are you going to do?' Tash asked me.

'Get better. Get my arm working again.'

'Can you? The doctors seem pretty sure you won't get the strength back, not fully.'

'What do doctors know? They don't know me.'

'Rob, we're sinking. You need a new career. You should study. You need a degree.'

'I've never needed a piece of paper before. I don't need one now,' I said stubbornly.

She wasn't giving up. 'How many times have I heard you say, "If you want a different result, you have to do something different"? You're not walking your talk.'

That hurt, because it was true. Knowing I was on weak ground, I started grasping at straws. 'I'm from the school of hard knocks, the university of life.' Even as those drab clichés left my mouth I knew I was being petulant; worse, a reverse snob.

'Really? Well that's not helping you, me or our children.'

'Steve Jobs and Richard Branson didn't need degrees.'

'You're right. I'm sorry to break this to you though; you're not Steve Jobs or Richard Branson.'

Distracted by the pain in my shoulder and scared my days of teaching unarmed combat could be coming to an end, I descended to adolescent whining. 'Is that what you want then? Steve Jobs or Richard Branson for a husband?'

'Steve Jobs refused to have anything to do with his daughter for the first two years of her life – her mother raised her on welfare. Richard Branson started his career selling counterfeit records and trying to cheat the British Customs' tax system. He was lucky not to go to jail.'

Keen to go off on a tangent, I exclaimed, 'How do you know that?'

'It's in his autobiography.'

I didn't have anywhere left to go.

'Rob, I don't want to be married to a billionaire. And I certainly don't want someone like Steve Jobs to be the father of my children. I want you,' Tash said gently.

I went for a walk. A long walk. My knee hurt, but the pain in my shoulder was worse. The prediction about nerve damage had to be accurate. A broken bone alone couldn't possibly generate this much pain. Even so, the physical pain was nothing compared to the agony of failing to be the husband and father I wanted to be for my wife and children. I was feeling very sorry for myself.

But while I was out walking, serendipity called. Tash was waiting with a message. 'A man called Geoff Crewe wants you to phone him.'

'Who is he?'

'He says he owns a financial planning company. He's read your book and he wants to talk to you about a presentation.'

'What kind of presentation?'

She shrugged. 'Why don't you call him and find out?'

The guy was direct and to the point. 'I liked your approach,' he said, 'and was wondering if you'd be prepared to deliver a keynote presentation at a business conference I'm organising.'

'A keynote presentation?' I had only the haziest notion of what a keynote presentation was.

'Yes. You'd need to talk for an hour or so.'

'What do you want me to talk about?' I was

struggling to see how my background would relate to a business audience.

'Some of the things you discuss in your book. Adaptability. Resilience. The pursuit of excellence.'

That was pretty ironic I thought, under the circumstances. Then again, maybe it was a sign. 'Where?' I asked cautiously. Though Crewe sounded okay there was always a possibility he was a nut case.

'The Gold Coast.'

I did the sums in my head. Travel to Queensland; accommodation for one, maybe two, nights; meals … it sounded as if the deal might cost me money.

'Are you … er … what are you thinking of paying?' I asked tentatively.

When he told me I had great difficulty in not yelling, 'What! How much? Travel and accommodation as well?' Instead, in what I hoped sounded like a calm voice I said, 'Yes, that's acceptable.'

And so, a few weeks later, I gave my first corporate presentation. I was a little nervous, but compared to teaching unarmed combat, public speaking is a walk in the park; there is no risk of physical injury and by that stage I'd worked out the keys to effective group communication. *Do not ever learn a speech verbatim*; avoid PowerPoint, and clichés, like the plague; use humour when appropriate; maintain eye contact with the people you want to convince; focus on the audience's needs, not your own; use stories to illustrate key points. Never swear … unless it's absolutely bloody necessary.

That first engagement led to another, and another. Pretty soon I was making a good living from corporate work. And despite the negative predictions, my shoulder recovered fairly well and I was able to start accepting invitations to teach unarmed combat to groups like the Belgium police and the Netherlands police. And so began a strange walk in two diametrically opposed worlds: high-risk reaction and professional speaking. Curiously, I enjoyed both. Each was so obviously different from the other, yet also subtly similar, and I enjoyed the physical and intellectual contrasts ... in fact, I found it quietly amusing to be chauffeured to a five-star resort one day and then a few days later to be sweating it out with a SWAT team in some grubby gymnasium.

In what seemed no time Natasha reached full term and was admitted to the John Hunter Hospital in Newcastle where she gave birth to Brontë, our daughter, in the same room where, eighteen months earlier, Blake had been born. It was a happy, wonderful time. Our family seemed complete. Now we had two girls, the eldest and the youngest, like bookends, complementing the three boys.

Four weeks later the unimaginable happened. Brontë contracted a viral lung infection that rapidly developed into a bacterial infection as well. Rushed to John Hunter, she was connected by serious-faced nurses to life support and assigned round-the-clock supervision. From the other side of the sterile glass Natasha and I stared wide-eyed and numb with fear at our baby, her small, vulnerable body attached to machines by grotesque tubes as she alternated between fits of frighteningly violent coughing and a drugged unconsciousness that so closely resembled death.

Only twice were Natasha and I, wearing sterile gowns and masks, allowed close to her. On those occasions, placing my finger in the palm of her tiny hand and bending to brush my masked lips against her ear, I whispered, 'It's me, your daddy. I love you.'

I had never felt so ineffectual. Like the wound opening before the knife, I was coming to understand the first horrific rule of parenthood; the worst thing that could possibly happen to me was never going to happen to *me*. It would happen to my children; it was happening to my daughter.

On the third day, pandemonium broke out in the ward where Brontë was being monitored: her tiny lungs had collapsed and, exhausted, she lacked the strength to take another breath. With six nurses in tow, she was rushed to Intensive Care where the on-duty specialist managed to revive her.

'I have to be frank with you,' the specialist said, 'two days ago we had another baby with exactly the same symptoms. Sadly, that baby died. I don't want to be the bearer of bad news, but I don't think your little girl is going to make it.'

These were truly devastating words – words that my wife refused to accept. 'He may be a doctor,' Natasha said, 'but that doesn't mean he knows her future!' There was no anger in her voice when she said this – just incredible love.

I wanted to make everything all right, but how could I? I wanted to be strong, to hold up for Natasha and the children. But how could I be strong when I was so powerless? 'For God's sake,' I wailed, 'I wish there was something we could *do*.'

'There is,' Tash said.

'What? Tell me. What?'

'We can pray.'

'Pray?'

'That's doing something, isn't it? As a matter of fact, it's doing a lot.'

First we prayed with the children and then, later, we prayed together in our room. Afterwards, she said, 'There, we did something.'

Curiously, I felt lighter, less weighed down. Nothing, absolutely nothing, had changed. Brontë still hovered between life and death, yet I felt better.

We prayed at every opportunity for nine days. If we slept at all I have no memory of it. On the tenth day Brontë turned around. She began to recover. We brought her home two days later; she was gurgling and seeking to suckle. Carrying her into the house with my tired, smiling wife and happy, noisy children I thought, *this is living*.

That night I crept into Brontë's room. She was asleep, breathing peacefully. Placing my finger in the palm of her hand, I whispered close to her ear, 'It's me, your daddy. I love you.'

***

From my first speaking engagement I found people in corporate audiences who would say things like, 'There's a lot of similarities between what you talk about and Robert Cialdini's research,' or 'You must be familiar with Daniel Goleman's work on emotional intelligence.' Other names that came up were Malcolm Gladwell, Daniel Kahneman, Dan Ariely and Stephen Covey. In fact, I'd never read anything by these people. I was familiar with classic research by behavioural scientists such as Stanley Milgram and Solomon Asch, but I realised I needed to broaden my research pool. So I did, and in the process developed a leadership program I called *Leadership Without Rank* – which included non-physical elements of Kontact, such as persuasive communication and, to quote Rudyard Kipling, how to 'keep your head when all about you are losing theirs and blaming it on you.'

As I continued to refine *Leadership Without Rank*, my business continued to gain traction. I started to receive invitations to present half-day and full-day professional development programs for staff and leadership teams from all sorts of industries. At first I was reluctant to accept some of the engagements; after all, what did I know about mining or information technology or banking? But the more I worked with different groups the more I realised that my material wasn't about any one industry; it was about people. Ian Lynass, who went on to become the CEO of BIS Industries, hired me to run multiple programs for his executives, and in the process of running those programs I continued to learn from the people I was interacting with. In some ways it was like doing an accelerated MBA: I was gaining direct insights into the challenges faced by business leaders and how they formulated solutions to those challenges.

After securing a particularly lucrative contract to present a series of *Leadership Without Rank* workshops to a financial services company I returned home to my family in Soldiers Point happily singing, 'We're outta here.'

Natasha and the children came running from the kitchen. 'What do you mean?' she said.

'I mean we're going to stop renting and buy our own house.'

We found a place on a nine-acre block in the hinterland of the Gold Coast with a creek, plenty of birdlife and the regular appearance of frilled-neck lizards, green tree frogs and even the occasional rock wallaby. The main veranda was huge, overlooking a spectacular valley filled with eucalypts and acacias. The view was glorious.

'So what do you think?' I asked as we surveyed it.

'I love it,' Natasha said. 'But it's a lot of money. Can we afford it?'

'No, not really.'

We moved in a few weeks later.

***

After 9/11, public interest in all things related to security increased dramatically. A NSW government organisation contacted me to conduct an audit of the personal defence training of its people. I spent several weeks working in the field with operators, looking at what they did and how they did it. To describe their training syllabus as woefully inadequate wouldn't come close to indicating how downright dangerous it was. It was one of the worst examples of trying to engineer unjustified confidence that I had ever seen. I wrote a detailed report dissecting exactly what was wrong and what needed to be done to correct the problems. I learnt later I'd actually been hired to validate their program, not critique it. The organisation had no intention of changing anything; what they wanted was a tick in a box, a pat on the back and a hearty, 'Well done and keep up the great work.' Not getting the feedback they wanted from me, they paid a suburban guru to tell them what they wanted to hear and then kept on doing exactly what they had been doing.

This was a watershed moment for me. Having proven the value of Kontact to groups like the FBI and the British SAS, I simply couldn't be bothered dealing with the ego and ignorance that too often go hand in glove with anything related to self-defence and unarmed combat. Apart from having some technical articles published in *Security Solutions* and the journal of the American Society for Law Enforcement Trainers, I decided to keep a relatively low profile in the security arena.

Even so, some months after the invasion of Iraq I started getting calls. Some were from people I knew, some from people who had heard about me. They were all about the same thing. Iraq. Private security companies, of which there were many, were paying top dollar to experienced people to provide protection to civilian workers in Iraq. Was I interested? I was not.

My fortieth birthday came and went, and my forty-first. I was making a comfortable living from corporate presentations and enjoying the process of applying *kaizen* to refine *Leadership Without Rank*. Life was good.

And then came the seventh of July and the London bombings.

Baghdad

It's funny how a little thing can change the course of your life; an unexpected phone call; a chance meeting; a passing comment; a moment spent choosing between turning left or turning right.

I'd just finished a sixty-minute keynote address for a group of computer technology managers. The presentation had gone well; the audience had laughed in all the right places, taken notes and generally had a good time. The conference organiser was pleased with the result and was in the process of briefing me for another event when one of the delegates approached. I could see by her body language that she was clearly 'on a mission'.

'Your talk was …' she paused, 'um, interesting.'

I paused too before saying, 'Um, thanks.' I don't think she got the joke.

'But, don't you think you're a bit young to retire from the real world?'

'What do you mean?' I asked, although I had a feeling I knew what was coming.

'If you've really got something to offer, what are you doing at a conference at a five-star resort?'

'You're at a conference at a five-star resort,' I said, keeping my tone light.

'Yes, but if I had your background and skills, I'd be helping aid-workers in Africa or something like that.'

'Last month I spent two weeks in Kenya providing personal safety training to field staff from UNICEF and World Vision.'

'You did?' She looked sceptical. 'You never said that in your speech.'

'There are lots of things I didn't say in my speech.'

'Well, I suppose you were well paid for it.'

'Actually, my trip to Kenya was voluntary. I didn't get paid a cent.'

That stumped her. She looked like she was searching for a reply, started to speak, stopped and then walked away. Whether she believed me or not was irrelevant to me. Everything I'd said was the truth.

In addition to mentors such as Andy Chalmers, one of the leaders I've learnt from during the course of my travels is Craig Kingston. After joining the army as a sixteen-year-old apprentice diesel mechanic, Craig progressed through the ranks to Lt. Colonel before transitioning to the corporate sector. A view Craig and I share is that when leaders or organisations focus myopically on being popular and become overly scared of making mistakes, there is a fundamental shift away from effectiveness. The same applies in the arena of public speaking. When a speaker becomes too concerned about having everyone like their message, something important is lost.

On the flight home I thought about the delegate's comments, but not for long. I subscribe to the view: 'I don't know the key to success, but the key to failure is trying to please everybody.'

The next day was the seventh of July. I watched the newscasts for hours; it was the longest time I'd sat in front of a television in years. I saw the bodies stretchered into the ambulances, the walking wounded, shocked and bloodily bandaged, being helped by emergency services people.

Adjusting to civilian life after military service can be challenging – especially if someone leaves the military because of health problems. In my case the injuries that led to my discharge were relatively minor, and yet what I missed most about the army was being measured by actions, not words. Watching the emergency workers dealing with the devastation in London, I was inspired. In the absence of any bolt of lightning, I decided that I would go to Iraq. I would go there and provide close personal protection to aid-workers in that country.

It's likely the conversation with the delegate the day before influenced my decision, but it's probable I would have reached the same conclusion anyway. Sometimes – not often, but sometimes – following a particular course of action just *feels* right. That doesn't mean that it feels *nice* or *easy*, but it does feel *right*. It would be possible to over-analyse that type of rationale, but for me it's a formula that works.

First I had to talk with Tash, who greeted my proposal with eyebrows raised.

'Iraq?' she said. 'Why ever would you want to work in Iraq?'

'An NGO is providing aid-workers to help in formulating the new Iraqi Constitution. It involves travelling around Baghdad, meeting with members of the different communities. The Shiites, the Sunnis, the Christians, the Kurds. They want experienced security operators to help in the process.'

'But surely Iraq is too dangerous right now?'

'We go in under the radar. Everything is low-profile. No uniforms. Civilian vehicles.'

'You're not answering my question, Rob. Iraq is dangerous, yes?'

'Yes, it is,' I admitted.

'Then why on earth would you even think about going there?'

'I want to make a contribution. In a small way I think I can make a positive difference.'

'Noble, but what about us?'

'It's us I'm thinking of. You know how I feel about life; it has to be lived. It's like parachuting; the only way to remove all risk from parachuting is to remove all elements that involve height.'

'Rob, I don't see what that has to do with us, and especially our children.'

'Look at it this way. As a parent, everything I do is an example. I can take easy, safe options and by default teach our children to be timid spectators of life. Or, I can use my skills in a way that demonstrates the value of getting off the sideline.'

'But what if you're injured, or worse?' The way Tash said 'or worse' wasn't lost on me. It was the trump card, I knew that. I'd been playing it since we'd become a family. I had no valid response, but I really wanted to go.

'I'm sorry, Tash, I just feel this is what I have to do.'

'I think there's something else going on,' she said, looking at me searchingly.

I didn't answer.

'Do you want to know what I think? I think you are still reacting to the way the army discharged you. I think it still bothers you.'

'I don't know,' I replied. I was thinking how she wasn't the first woman to have made that connection. I felt embarrassed, and dropped my gaze. If I was rebelling from an old sense of grievance, I should have moved on. But the fact was I still had an itch that needed to be scratched. Unable to find words to continue the conversation, I found myself thinking about sitting in the front seat of a Buick in Los Angeles with Jerry beside me, telling me how he only ever wanted one career.

After a long pause Tash said, 'I don't really understand. Maybe it's because I'm a woman, or maybe it's because it wasn't my career that was taken from me. Either way, it doesn't matter. If going to Iraq is important to you, it's important to me.'

The generosity of her response almost made me change my mind. She was being a far better spouse than me.

'When?' she asked.

'The sooner I go, the sooner I'll be back.'

'Well then, you'd better get packing,' she said, and wrapped her arms around me.

Some months earlier I'd received an email from Greg Shaw, the man who got me the Sydney Olympics work with SOCOG, saying that he was managing a security company in Iraq and offering me a job running advanced defensive tactics training for his operatives. I called his mobile number. He seemed pleased to hear from me.

'Where are you?' I asked.

'Sitting in a compound in Baghdad listening to small-arms fire and a few mortars going off,' he said casually. 'Situation normal.'

'I was thinking if you have a job for me I might come out there for a bit.'

'Yeah? That'd be great. Right now I could offer you work training Iraqis as bodyguards for the new Iraqi magistrates. The money's probably not what you get as a corporate fat-cat, but it's still good; our budget is healthy and I could make it worth your while.'

'Actually, I was thinking of something more like providing security for civilian aid-workers.'

'Really? Well, I should tell you that's far more dangerous. With the training job you'd spend most of your time inside the compound, whereas in a protection unit you're right out there – on the streets.'

'How dangerous is dangerous?'

There was a moment's silence. 'We lost our first man last month.'

'What happened?'

'Suicide bomber. We were conducting an escort from Baghdad airport, sandwiched between two US Embassy convoys. Our guys were in the middle of the fleet and bore the brunt of the blast. One was killed on impact; one has both his legs broken, another has serious burns to thirty-five per cent of his body.'

I thought about it, picturing the scene. After what must have been a while I heard Greg's voice, 'Hello, hello, you still there?'

'Yeah, I'm here. So who are your men?'

'Aussies mainly, ex-special forces and state cops. We've also got a few former French Foreign Legionnaires along with a handful of Brits, some Canadians, a few other nationalities. They all know their business. So, what do you think?'

It took another long moment for me to decide. 'I'd like a short-term contract, say three months.'

Greg's tone grew serious. 'Are you fit?' How's your shoulder?'

'Fine. I clocked up three kilometres in the pool this morning.'

'Good.' His tone was dark. 'Because you'll need to be fit; as fit as you've ever been. Physically and mentally. Nothing you could possibly imagine is going to prepare you for this place.'

It took me a couple of frenetic weeks to organise my affairs, including some awkward moments returning advance fees I'd received for corporate engagements I was now having to cancel. Most clients understood that I had security commitments that had to take priority, but a few couldn't see why I would risk my neck for less money than I could earn as a speaker. I wasn't entirely sure I understood myself; all I knew was that there was a cost to what I was doing and it wasn't only pecuniary.

The night before I was due to fly out I lay on the bed with our youngest children reading them a story. To finish I turned out the lights and, in the darkness, recited *The Man From Snowy River* (which they called the Horse Story). Confident that they were all asleep I was about to creep away when out of the blackness a voice whispered, 'You will come back, won't you Daddy?' The innocent directness of the question no-one else had dared ask punched me in the heart.

Before I could speak another small but confident voice came out of the darkness. 'Of course he will. Daddy loves us. He always comes back.' Gulping, I bent to kiss the owner of the second voice, smelling the warm sweetness of a child falling asleep, sensing the movement as the little body nestled itself for the night. 'You *will* come back, won't you Daddy?' the first voice whispered plaintively.

'Of course I will,' I murmured. 'I always come back.'

I stumbled into the bathroom, sat on the edge of the bath and breathed deeply, barely holding back tears. Had I told the truth? Would I come back or would those words turn out to be the worst lie a child could hear?

After a while I stood up, splashed cold water on my face and walked as nonchalantly as I could into the lounge. Natasha looked up from her place on the sofa. 'You look upset,' she said.

It was the beginning of a long conversation. Afterwards we both felt better.

***

The connection from Dubai into Iraq was on Ishta Airlines flight XV101. I stared down as the plane came in over Baghdad, spiralling down in a series of tight corkscrews to confuse the aim of any insurgents with ground-to-air missiles. All I could see was sand, a few drooping date palms and a sea of box-like houses, some big, some small, each one the same dull, drab colour; a colour which, I realised as we dropped lower, was not paint but dust. Not the sienna-red dust of the central Australian desert, but a flat, lifeless grey.

A pall of smoke hung over the city, in the centre of which I glimpsed the winding Tigris flowing north to south and shining like a silver snake.

Greg was waiting for me in the arrivals lounge. 'Welcome to Baghdad,' he said, shaking my hand warmly.

I grinned. 'It's great to see you again.' I glanced around, mildly surprised. The place was better than I'd expected: the floor well polished; the rows of plastic seating that somehow reminded me of McDonald's, clean and, apart from a few cigarette burns, well maintained. As well as a few uniformed soldiers there were close to a dozen clusters of private security contractors standing around waiting to collect clients.

Outside, the heat hit me like a hammer, the dust immediately getting into my eyes and mouth. 'This place is bloody dusty,' Greg said. 'It's a bugger, but you learn to live with it.'

I blinked rapidly, noticing the airport walls and entrances heavily sandbagged, the windows taped, the ground littered with discarded plastic water bottles swirling about in the wind. Staring through the dazzling sunshine I saw concrete barriers and rolls of razor wire everywhere.

One of Greg's men handed me a Kevlar jacket murmuring, 'There you go, buddy. You gotta be armoured up for the trip.' I put it on.

Greg briefed me.

'Okay. We'll be travelling the first few kilometres in relative security as the roads leading to and from the airport are well protected by the Yanks and act as a kind of buffer zone. Then we pass a checkpoint and after that we are on the most dangerous stretch of road on the planet. It's sixteen kilometres east to the Green Zone in Baghdad and the score so far is about two dead for every hundred metres. It's a battle zone. Insurgents open up on us with armour-piercing grenades, missile launchers, machine-guns, mortars, land mines, plus a lot of VBIEDs.'

I didn't understand the last term. 'Veebee-i-e-dees?'

'That's vehicle-borne improvised explosive devices. What the media calls car bombs. One of which killed our bloke halfway along the road. So, we drive fast, like we're in a hurry. Intimidation, that's the name of the game here. Something gets in our way we drive over it or through it. Okay?'

'Okay.'

'Good.' He led the way into a concrete-covered parking lot also liberally scattered with dust and plastic water bottles, stopping at three armoured LandCruisers, two of which, with their tailgates in the open position, were adapted to accommodate rear gunners. There was a sign attached to the back of one of the vehicles and I stepped around to take a look. In English it read: DANGER! STAY BACK 100M. DEADLY FORCE AUTHORISED! Additional Arabic writing on the sign presumably said the same thing.

I shot an enquiring glance at Greg. 'It means what it says,' he said simply. 'Standard rules of engagement; if any vehicle comes within a hundred metres we flash a spotlight at it. If that doesn't deter it, we fire a warning shot into the road a few metres in front of the vehicle. If that doesn't do it, the next round is fired into the vehicle's grille. The round is armour piercing, it'll go through the engine block.'

'And if that doesn't stop them?'

'The protocol is to shoot the driver in the head.'

'Ever had to do it?'

He shook his head. 'Never had to do more than fire in the road. Most vehicles get the hell out of the way when they see a convoy. Why wouldn't they? They can't exactly miss us – matching SUVs, obviously armoured, darkened windows, driving fast and in formation. We're high-profile and hard-core. We stick out like dogs' balls.'

'What about other convoys?'

'The American and British military convoys apply the same rules. A hundred-metre bubble, no exceptions. Out on the road we all enforce the exclusion zone. They stay away from us. We stay away from them. Same with most of the other PMCs.'

I had just landed in a war zone. I realised I'd need to get up to speed on the jargon.

'PMCs?'

'Private Military Companies – more euphemistically known as PSCs: Private Security Companies.'

'How many of those are there?'

'About three hundred.'

'That many?'

'And we're all busy. Twenty-six million people in this country, mate, and it's half the size of New South Wales. Five million just in Baghdad. That's a million more than Sydney. There's a lot to do here and there's a lot of people who don't want us to do it. Prepared to kill us and themselves to stop us. Anyway, we'd better get going.'

He reached into the back of the vehicle and came out with an AK47, which he handed to me.

I got in the back of the middle vehicle with the guy who had given me the body armour. Greg climbed in beside the driver. The vehicle had a left-hand drive.

Peering through the front window I watched the rear gunner in the lead vehicle scramble into position and wedge himself in, a Kalashnikov PKM across his lap. Moving slowly, the convoy negotiated the concrete barriers, Greg acknowledging the US soldiers guarding the airport approaches. We drove in a normal fashion for a few minutes until we passed what was evidently the airport's final checkpoint. The moment we were on the open road the driver shoved the pedal to the deck, forcing me back in my seat with the acceleration.

I gazed through the front window at the highway, a light dusting of sand blowing across the dark, pitted bitumen. Everywhere there were bomb craters and burnt-out cars, some of the craters pitting the road itself, the drivers swerving at speed to avoid them.

Greg was reading my mind. 'It's usually too dangerous to repair the road.' He indicated the groves of flattened palm trees on either side of the highway, beyond them a bleached landscape of scrubby desert, white cement walls and washed-out, Saddam-era housing blocks. 'The Yanks bulldozed the trees. They were providing cover for snipers and mortar crews.'

No airport road was attractive, but this was both gnarled and menacing, made all the more so by the occasional tank-like Bradley fighting vehicle parked by the side of the highway. On the other side of the median strip I watched an American convoy of Humvees rocketing towards us like artillery shells. It passed in a storm of dust and noise.

The guy beside me, an American, caught the look on my face and chuckled. 'Not too pretty, eh? The Yellow Brick Road this is not. But then, this ain't Kansas, Dorothy.'

I laughed. It seemed as good a response as any.

The Green Zone

After about twenty minutes the convoy turned north and crossed the river, cruising over a shell-scarred bridge that Greg announced was the Fourteenth of July Bridge, the main entry point from the airport into the Green Zone.

Inside the LandCruiser I felt the tension wind down. Gazing out of the windows I could see why. Surrounded by four-metre-high reinforced blast-proof concrete slabs that Greg called T-walls, the area was defended by long coils of razor wire, chain-link fences and large earthen berms, its armed checkpoints monitored by M1 Abrams tanks, Bradley fighting vehicles and Humvees, topped off with .50 calibre machine-guns. The place looked under siege – the ultimate gated community. We drove through the streets to Camp Freedom, the headquarters of the US Army's 3rd Infantry Division, situated on the banks of the Tigris.

'Okay, this is home for the next week,' Greg told me as we got out of the vehicles. 'You'll be undergoing refresher training here.'

'What's that involve?'

'Pistol, rifle and machine-gun assessment. Plus of course tactical driving, first aid, radio communications … the whole bag of tricks. Actually, the week is more in the nature of an evaluation. Everybody who arrives here is expected to possess good skills already. But you'll need to pass. Everyone has to pass evaluation, or their life-insurance cover is invalid. For you it'll be a piece of cake.'

'Who's doing the evaluation? The Yanks?'

'No, our own people. We merely get to live on Uncle Sam's real estate and use the facilities – the weapons range, gymnasium, canteen and so on. Beyond that we're self-sufficient.'

Greg showed me to my bungalow – an aluminium demountable, similar to mining-camp accommodation – then took me on a quick tour of the camp's facilities. That afternoon I was issued with a Serbian-made CZ99 pistol and the Swiss SG552 assault rifle. As I was examining the weapons the armourer said, 'We'll be evaluating you on your handling skills tomorrow morning.'

I glanced up in alarm, Greg's nonchalant faith in my competency flying out the window. Weapons handling is essentially a question of familiarity and practice. While I had maintained marksmanship skills since leaving South Africa, I had neither handled nor even seen the particular weapons now in front of me.

'Tomorrow?' I repeated in a hollow tone.

The armourer's face was stony. 'Yup.'

That evening I returned to my bungalow with the weapons and spent most of the night teaching myself how to strip and assemble them as well as practising stoppage drills. By the time I got to bed in the early hours my fingers were bleeding. At the evaluation the following morning, the instructor said, 'I'll show you once, then you do it with me. Try to keep up.' In fact I beat him, on both the pistol and the assault rifle.

My final test was to strip and reassemble the SG552 blindfolded. As I was trying to join the connecting pin with the trigger housing and the stock, I fumbled and dropped the weapon. 'Oops,' I said.

'Oops? What the fuck is oops?' the instructor snarled.

I had to smile. I'd become used to having my children around me and thus modifying my language. But this was a war zone, and when you dropped your weapon, the thing that might conceivably save your life or the life of people you worked with, it was probably not typical to say oops.

Eating in the canteen surrounded by US soldiers I was pleasantly surprised by the absence of stereotypes. The men were restrained, friendly and helpful.

I watched them preparing to go out on patrol, knowing it would soon be my turn to leave the comparative safety of the Green Zone. On a map of Baghdad the Green Zone was scarcely three kilometres square, nestled in a curving loop of the river's west bank that looked exactly like the belly of a pregnant woman. Which was appropriate, I thought. There was a safe, womblike quality to the Green Zone. Here it was almost a slice of Little

America; I could get take-away pizzas, Burger King fries and Baskin Robbins ice cream. Outside, the rest of the city was a cruel, threatening, and often bloody world.

Not for nothing was the outside called the Red Zone.

My instructors took great pains in schooling me in the rules of engagement, especially as they applied to suicide bombers. There were a lot of subtle signs that telescoped into those final rules of shooting into a vehicle's grille, then shooting the driver in the head. Like all risk, the level of threat from possible VBIEDs had to be assessed.

As in any war, resources were scarce and the enemy presumably considered suicide bombers a finite commodity, not to be wasted unnecessarily. Therefore, any car containing only the driver was reckoned a higher-level risk than one with passengers. Similarly, because bombs and their metal casings were heavy, cars travelling low to the ground were considered risky – although bombers had been known to put manikins in their cars and to fit heavy shock absorbers to mask the weight of their vehicles.

I listened intently to the briefing sessions and took careful note of the signs to watch for, but I knew much of my decision would come from my instinct. Not just my eyes but my gut would tell me when something wasn't right.

They showed me a video of a recent small-arms ambush by insurgents on the Baghdad

International Air Port road (BIAP). The footage had been recorded with a camcorder attached to the dashboard of the second SUV – a common practice in most convoys. I watched it dispassionately, listening to the instructor's critique. Bereft of Hollywood finesse – perfect lighting, loud, colourful explosions, sustained machine-gun fire – the video's poor quality made it seem amateurish, almost boring. Except that it was real and I was watching an event in which men just like me had been shot to death.

The footage showed the lead SUV, about eighty metres ahead, being hit. Rounds were kicking up the tarmac around it and, when I looked closely, smacking into its side. They were coming from a clump of date palm stumps off to the right. The lead vehicle stopped, presumably incapacitated, and the operators inside had, the instructor intoned in his low, steady voice-over, 'cracked the doors,' which meant they had chosen to open the vehicle doors in what may have been an attempt to drag a body out to administer first aid while others tried to return fire. As this was happening the second vehicle, now also stationary, was also taking fire. Above the loud noise of the idling engine, I heard sporadic, three and four-round bursts of gunfire, followed by what seemed a long pause before another burst. Someone in the second vehicle, possibly the driver, was shouting, doing his best to reassure one of his team who, I guessed, had 'cracked a door' to engage the insurgents and been shot.

Moments later I saw a man, again probably the driver, entering the frame in front of the bonnet from the left, bend down and begin dragging what had to be a wounded man backwards. I watched the driver's face contort and his shoulders hunch as he took up the weight and started shuffling backwards, alternately looking down to speak to the wounded man and looking up towards the incoming fire.

Moments later something or someone bumped the camera and it fell on its side, giving the rest of the sequence a weird perspective. Then, before the ambush was over, the camera was knocked again and everything went black. Like death.

The sequence had lasted no more than four minutes, and when the screen went dark I heard the instructor murmur, 'There but for the grace of God go I.'

They made me watch the video repeatedly, analysing the footage, learning what had gone wrong, and by the time I'd watched it for the eighth or ninth time I had come to know every date palm stump and shell hole in the tarmac surrounding the area of contact. It was the most disconcerting training video I'd ever watched. At the end of the week, after I had passed all the evaluation tests, Greg took me to the US Embassy; in the heart of the Green Zone, the building it occupied had been one of Saddam's palaces, which even included an official throne room. In what turned out to be a lengthy process

I was fingerprinted, photographed and issued with a US Department of Defense Contractor ID card, which allowed me to pass US military checkpoints in both the Green and Red Zones, enter US military bases throughout Iraq, receive emergency medical treatment at military field hospitals, fly on military helicopters, and buy tax-exempt goods from the military PX stores.

I felt like I had come full circle and was a soldier once more.

I was briefed on my first assignment and convoyed to a compound in Karadah in the Red Zone. This would be my new home. As the driver moved the four-tonne armoured vehicle past the gates I surveyed the place. It looked like a fortress. Surrounded by the ubiquitous blast-proof concrete T-walls, it was protected by a set of huge metal gates, watchtowers with heavy machine-guns and machine-gun nests on many of the roofs.

Sleeping accommodation for those of us in the security detail was in a three-storey villa in the heart of the compound.

I chose a room overlooking a brick wall. Once a normal-sized room, it had been partitioned down the middle to create a storeroom on the other side. There was a mattress on the floor, a desk, a chair and a cupboard. There were no curtains. I chose it because it was tucked around a couple of odd corridors, which meant if the compound was stormed in the early hours I'd have more time to respond to the sound of gunfire. About a dozen guys slept in the villa, with two bathrooms between us.

After settling in, which took no more than a couple of minutes, one of the guys on my team showed me the canteen, where I had a quick meal. Afterwards the same guy led me downstairs to The Pit, the compound's pub located in the basement of the hotel where the clients stayed. I ordered myself a soft drink and stood at the bar with some of the men from my company. I liked the atmosphere, the air buzzing with that unique sense of excitement generated by a random mix of expats thrown together in a foreign country.

My first convoy was the following day. Its mission was to return a group of aid-workers to the airport along the sixteen kilometres of road the US military called Route Irish, or Irish for short. I never knew for sure why; the best explanation I heard was that, supposedly, the *Guinness Book of Records* had named it the most dangerous stretch of road in the world.

Returning from the airport, I was riding in the lead car next to the driver. Suddenly, over the sound of the big V8 engine, I heard the dull thump of mortars somewhere to our left. I peered past the driver, an ex-Legionnaire. He glanced at me and shrugged as only a Frenchman could. The shrug said it all.

That afternoon I went on another convoy, the following day two more; within a week I was adapting to the rhythm of my new life.

What I found most difficult was adjusting to the country itself.

First, the place was seriously hot. The Americans measured temperature in Fahrenheit and I had arrived on a cool day: 90°F. Since then the thermometer had risen to 114°F and stayed there, every day the same, a dry, blistering heat. Although I preferred a dry heat to the humidity of PNG, it brought its own problems, primarily that choking, sandy dust that got everywhere. Outside, dust coated everything; inside a thin film of it covered the floors, tables, chairs, drink bottles. I spent a lot of time stripping my weapons and cleaning them.

On top of the heat and the dust, the city was one giant garbage dump. Before the wars and sanctions, Baghdad had been a sophisticated city, but those days were long gone. Now the Iraqis threw their domestic rubbish out on the road in front of their apartment blocks, and when the giant heaps of plastic water bottles, Coke cans and disposable nappies got too big, someone doused them with petrol and set light to them. There were fires burning all the time, not only from the garbage, but from bombs and from the sabotaged oil pipelines that burnt for days. A permanent pall hung over the city, smudging the sun in noxious smoke.

Beyond the constant smoke and dust, noisy and smelly generators made Iraq a difficult place to even breathe in. The city appeared to have no state-run electricity grid; instead there were thousands upon thousands of diesel generators ranging from the size of Eskys to some the size of trucks, every one belching out billows of black exhaust fumes.

Baghdad, the fabled city of the Arabian tales I had read to my children, was smashed and wasted, with bomb craters too dangerous to repair in the roadways, and enormous holes puncturing the roofs and walls of once magnificent homes and palaces. Everywhere there was razor wire; everywhere the four-metre, blast-proof T-walls. There were rows and rows of T-walls, like some maniacal gigantic maze.

The city was ugly, toxic and perilous, the danger continually reasserted by the *boom* of bombs, the *crump* of mortars and the seemingly constant *whump-whump-whump* of helicopters – medical helicopters transporting the wounded, Blackhawks moving troops, even AH64 Apache gunships on combat missions. And always there were incidents – sixty-seven a day on average – small-arms and mortar attacks on the airport road; an Iraqi suicide bomber blowing up a fuel tanker at a crowded market, killing himself and ninety-one other people while wounding a further hundred and sixty; another suicide bomber targeting an American army patrol that stopped to hand out candy to the locals. The body count from that one included twenty-four dead Iraqi children.

Years before I had struggled through Dante's *Divine Comedy*. Now, I told myself, I needn't have bothered. I was getting firsthand experience of the seven circles of hell. Iraq was its own Inferno.

Yet after a couple of weeks in the country, like most operators I had settled in. I had learnt more lingo and discovered that, as a member of a PMC, I was a PSD or Personnel Security Detail, which meant I was a non-uniformed security contractor. PSD was practically a rank; all freelance security operators were members of a definite tribe.

I am proud to say that I never saw an Australian or Kiwi speak disrespectfully or abusively to an Iraqi – which is more than I could say for some of the Eastern Europeans. This was an observation, not prejudice, but some of those guys would have been better off staying home and cleaning toilets. Most of them were ex-Legionnaires, although you wouldn't have guessed it – the French Foreign Legion was a top military unit, with high standards and good discipline. But now these guys were out of the Legion some of them clearly didn't believe that ongoing discipline was necessary. It wouldn't matter, except that I was going out on convoy with these people.

One afternoon, returning from the airport on Route Irish, one of them, a Bulgarian ex-Legionnaire called Mick, who reminded me of Milo in Alice Springs, tried to persuade me that if a convoy was ambushed from its right and the vehicles could not be driven away, then the PSDs should get out on the *right-hand side* of the vehicles to return fire, thus proving they were not scared of the enemy.

Concentrating on keeping tight formation with the SUVs ahead, I gave him the standard perspective: 'It's much smarter to get out on the opposite side and move into a position where we can return fire using the vehicle as optical and, to some, extent, ballistic cover,' I said. 'Tactically, that's the only thing to do.'

'Ha,' the Bulgarian sneered, 'that shows you scared.'

'So?'

There was no point in wasting my breath. This idiot was not only stupid, he was childish with it. Sitting up front next to me he had the extremely annoying habit of resting the muzzle of his AK47 on the toe of his boot and playing with the trigger with the safety off and a round up the chamber. I was disappointed he didn't pull the trigger. But, the Bulgarian was an exception. Most of the guys I found myself working with were competent professionals.

One lunchtime I was chatting with Stan, a Fijian, and Keith, a Kiwi from a room close to mine. The big Kiwi was telling a story of life in Iraq.

'I was at the airport,' he said. 'Had just seen some NGO aid-workers off when I spotted this civilian woman getting off a flight. She was on her own.'

'Alone?' Stan repeated.

'Right. You *never* see that here. She was wandering about the place like she was at John F Kennedy or Heathrow … not Baghdad bloody airport. So I went up to her and asked how she was planning to get to the city. She said she was going to take a taxi. She thought she could take a cab like she was still in the Netherlands. Anyway, I told her how that was about the most dangerous thing she could do in Iraq. But she wouldn't believe me, seemed offended even that I should be telling her that. She said all the media hype about violence was just American propaganda. I offered to take her in the convoy. She wouldn't have it.'

He stopped and looked up. Two Apache gunships in combat formation were coming in low over the rooftops about a kilometre away. We watched as the lead chopper opened fire, the smoke trails of two rockets – one red, one green – shooting down towards the hidden target. For a few moments the gunships hovered, then they banked and headed north. Keith waited for the noise to die away before continuing. No-one commented on the action. It was too familiar.

'Go on,' I said.

'Well, she must have left the airport before we did because about ten minutes down Route Irish we came across her taxi. It had been ambushed and the woman was standing beside it. In flames. She was melting in a ball of flame. She was screaming and melting ... screaming and melting.' He stopped.

We waited.

'I've got two regrets,' he said. 'One, I didn't force her to join our convoy. Two, I didn't put a bullet in her head as I watched her melt and listened to her scream.'

The Red Zone

It was a busy day. In the morning we had escorted some people from the State University of New York out of the Red Zone and into the Green Zone; in the afternoon we took a group of NGO personnel along BIAP to the airport. Members of the NGO group were pleased to be getting out: they had been in the country for months.

One young guy, his face grey and with dark rings under his eyes, was explaining the mitigation of risk and the Pareto principle to us PSDs in the vehicle: eighty per cent of the risk in Iraq was located in twenty per cent of the country, while a hundred per cent of the risk came from less than ten per cent of the population. He had a whole raft of formulae concerning risk. Time was also a factor. Risk moved in correlation to time and exposure: the longer the exposure the greater the risk. Which was why he was glad to be getting out. He had worked out that with the time he had been in Iraq, he was now at maximum risk. Of course, he would have been at no risk of being killed or maimed if he had never come here, he said. But having come, his chances of being killed increased every day.

Danger comes closer with time.

I thought of mortar bombs creeping closer and ever closer to their target and wondered where I stood on the Pareto scale. In the time I had been in Iraq one security operative from another PMC had been killed, two others wounded.

On the return trip in the afternoon, I took up position as rear gunner, wedging myself in as best I could and settling the PKM on my lap. A few kilometres along BIAP a blue sedan containing a lone driver joined the freeway from a slip road. The sedan would have to have gone through at least one Iraqi police roadblock to get onto Route Irish, but that wasn't much comfort to me. I watched it carefully. It closed on the convoy rapidly and within seconds was nudging our hundred-metre exclusion zone.

I waved the driver off, pointing to the Land-Cruiser's warning sign and energetically flashing a white strobe light at him. But the sedan kept coming. Now it was well inside the bubble. I waved another couple of times then raised the machine-gun in an obviously threatening manner. At seventy metres the driver must have seen me, but still the sedan failed to slow down. I fired into the bitumen in front of the vehicle, the round kicking up a spout of black tarmac, easily visible to the driver. He took no notice.

I felt my heartbeat notching up.

The car was fifty metres off and closing fast. I raised the weapon and fired an armour-piercing round into the vehicle's grille, before immediately sighting the weapon for the next shot. Through the driver's head. At this range I wouldn't miss. But the car was spinning off the bitumen road onto the sandy shoulder, disappearing in a storm of dust. The convoy kept moving.

I peered into the dust. Had I hit the driver? The round would have penetrated the engine block and blown the engine, but would it have gone beyond that? I didn't know.

The question that really consumed me was whether or not he was a bomber. If the guy wasn't a suicide bomber, why had he not heeded the blindingly obvious warnings? Another second or two and I would have squeezed the trigger.

Back at the compound I wrote up an incident report for the duty-watch keeper. When I'd finished I stared at the bald statement of the facts. Incident reports, I reflected, were not about feelings, and duty-watch keepers, like today's ex-Royal Marine Sergeant, were definitely not interested in the philosophical reflections of their authors. Yet making out an incident report was one measure of the changing magnitude of risk.

Two days later I completed another report.

Travelling back on Route Irish from the airport towards the Green Zone, I was driving the lead LandCruiser when I found my side of the highway blocked by a US army convoy of Humvees responding to an explosion a few hundred metres ahead. I slowed to a crawl and had to stop – the hairs prickling on the back of my neck. The last thing anybody ever wanted to do on BIAP was stop. We were now sitting ducks for any sniper or mortar crew hidden in the suburbs beyond the road. And traffic was coming up behind us.

Getting on the radio to the other drivers, I initiated the standard tactic for a blocked BIAP, driving aggressively forward for thirty metres then reversing the same distance; forward again, then back, forward and back, thus presenting at least a partially moving target to any insurgents. For a couple of minutes it worked, though a couple of minutes of BIAP time seemed to stretch into half a lifetime of heartbeats.

But oncoming traffic was edging forward, reducing our room to manoeuvre down to twenty metres … fifteen … ten … until we were wedged in.

I glanced about, trying to figure the next course of action. The scene outside the vehicle was the same as it was everywhere; pitted, potholed tarmac and truncated date palms. Nothing remarkable. Except …

A chill went down my spine. This was where the ambush had taken place. I'd watched the training video enough times and since then had driven BIAP often enough to know every sawn-off date palm, every hole and crevice in the road.

Suddenly, flickering on my windscreen, I saw poorly lit images of an SUV eighty metres ahead taking fire from a clump of date palm stumps to my right. I jerked back in my seat, shocked and disorientated. I felt my hands go clammy, less from fear of what was happening outside than from what was going on inside my head as I saw again the footage I'd watched in training. Not only was I in a dangerous situation that was completely real, wedged in on BIAP, my mind was also being sucked into another that was unreal – images from a situation I had studied via a dead man's camcorder. I 'saw' men crack the doors in the vehicle in front; 'saw' the short bursts of gunfire smacking into my own vehicle. Two independent dramas were occurring simultaneously.

It was as if I'd moved through the windscreen of the SUV and *into the video*. I wasn't here; I was there. And I was also somewhere ethereal and elevated, *watching myself not being here*. It was like watching a dramatic news event and then stepping through the screen into it.

The feeling was so bizarre, so surreal, it made my skin crawl.

I shook my head, forcing myself to focus on the reality, the here and now. I needed a solution – a way out. Now.

'Plan B,' I called into the radio and yanked the steering wheel, peeling the SUV out of the traffic and on to the median strip – leading the convoy into yet another danger zone.

BIAP's median strip was no more than a broad strip of dust, sand and the sawn-off stumps of date palms, on which some locals kept goats and even sowed a few crops. Crops were not the only things sown; insurgents planted landmines there and a few PSD and military convoys had been blasted crossing the strip.

The blockage on BIAP may have been a deliberate ploy, a strategy to induce a convoy to do exactly what I was now doing – drive across the strip and over a landmine powerful enough to destroy a four-tonne armoured SUV and either kill me or, at the very least, blow my legs off. And all I could do was drive, hoping like crazy I didn't hit a mine, while the two following SUVs followed *very* carefully in my tracks.

We made it, bouncing off the strip and onto the opposite side of the highway, driving *into* the stream of traffic. I switched on the siren, palmed the horn and started flashing the lights. The traffic coming at us was thick and fast; above the sounds of the siren and our own horn I could hear the angry klaxons of approaching cars as I swerved from side to side to avoid bomb craters.

Sean, the guy up front beside me, had been a marksman with the British paras. He was Irish, with an accent so thick that most of the time I had no idea what he was saying, the only word I recognised with any certainty being 'facking'. There was a lot of facking now, with Sean screaming through the loudspeaker at the traffic barrelling towards us, '*Gitootdafackinwee, gitootdafackinwee.*'

My heart hammered as the adrenalin rocketed through my system. At any moment I was about to have a head-on collision.

Suddenly Sean opened his door and leant out into the rushing air, hanging from the vehicle by a strap he had looped around the hinges of the door. 'What in hell are you doing?' I yelled as Sean proceeded to raise his weapon and fire off three rounds.

The weapon was a Heckler & Koch G3, loaded with 7.62 tracer. Despite myself, despite the pumping rush of adrenalin and the need to focus on the road, I stared at the red tracers languidly flying over the roofs of the approaching vehicles. I found it easy to be captivated by tracer – manufactured with a phosphorescent coating, they burn brightly and allow the shooter to follow the flight path of the projectile to aid in the aiming process. Sean fired more warning shots, this time in front of the vehicles. I was irresistibly drawn to following their graceful flight, seeing their brilliant glow turn into something far more vicious as they exploded into the bitumen and ricocheted out of sight into the distance.

The traffic in front of us slewed onto the shoulder of the highway.

I felt my palms damp and spongy on the steering wheel. Although tracer fired into the roadway was effective for most oncoming traffic, it would never deter an American convoy of Humvees or Bradleys. The Yanks would immediately assume we were insurgents and apply the first principle of defence against an oncoming vehicle. They would shoot the driver, me, in the head.

My gut clenched as I thought about it, my eyes straining for the familiar sight of Humvees approaching at speed, realising they might be the last thing I ever saw.

We drove on the wrong side of Route Irish for over a kilometre before I decided we could cross back to our own side of the highway. I indicated my intention and bounced on to the median strip, taking the convoy back into the potential minefield. We reached our own side of the highway where, with one hand on the wheel, I leant over and dragged Sean back inside the SUV. He slammed his door. '*Datwosfackingreet*,' he laughed.

We got back to the compound in the middle of the afternoon. The villa was quiet and I had a long shower, the water, as usual, whether from the hot or cold tap, lukewarm. Then I called Tash and the children from my room on my mobile phone. I considered telling her about the day's events, but decided it could only add to her worry. It was just good to hear her voice.

Later, I came down and was making my way across the dusty compound towards the canteen when a convoy from another PMC drove in. From time to time other convoys came in to refuel. I watched them clambering out of the armoured Range Rovers, the men carrying AK47s and encumbered by flak jackets and vests festooned with radios, smoke grenades and ammunition clips. Then I did a double take as I saw a guy getting out of the passenger side of the lead vehicle. There was no mistaking that squat figure or that ravaged face. Pug-ugly was still pug-ugly.

'Jocko?'

The little guy looked directly at me. 'Red? Fookin' hell, is that you?' He frowned, his face as ugly as a troll's. 'What the fook happened to your hair, ya bald prick?'

My world was suddenly filled with crazy Celts. 'Nice to see you too.' I crossed to the vehicles and we shook hands warmly.

'How are you?'

Jocko grinned. With his crooked teeth it wasn't a pretty sight. 'Never been better, mate. Should've known you'd be here.'

'Yeah? Why's that?'

'This is your kind of place.'

What kind of person did Jocko think I was if he thought Iraq was my kind of place?

'So, you want a drink?'

'Yer, a quick one.'

I took him downstairs to The Pit where I ordered myself a 7Up. Jocko asked for a light beer. He, too, in his own way, was being cautious. He'd been in the country eighteen months, he told me.

I asked whether, in that time, he thought things had got any better. That morning an Australian politician had been reported in the media as saying, 'The situation in Iraq is improving significantly.' The comment had been picked up by numerous news websites and seemed to be regarded as fact.

'Fookin' pollies, what do they know?' Jocko

snarled. 'Things might be improving when you're sitting behind a desk in Canberra. But here it's definitely getting worse.' He told me he had been involved in High-Profile convoys since arriving in Iraq. At first, incidents had been rare. Now he and his team were writing up incident reports too often for comfort. During his time two of the guys he'd worked with had been killed, four others seriously wounded.

'Sounds like you're pushing your luck, Jocko,' I said seriously.

He looked unfazed. 'Nah, I'll be right. Anyway, what about you?'

'Me?'

'Last time I saw you was in Alice Springs. What have you been up to since then?'

I told him about PNG, Kontact, South Africa, marriage, and the speaking circuit.

'You've done all right. I reckoned you might. Better than becoming a Rupert, eh?' he laughed.

I laughed with him. 'We've both come a long way since then, that's for sure.'

We chatted for a while before he glanced at his watch. 'I'd better get back. We've got a mission.'

We shook hands at the bar. This time we did exchange contact details. When Jocko wasn't in Iraq he lived in Thailand, and I fully intended to catch up with him if I ever found myself in that part of the world. 'Good luck. And take it easy, mate.'

He smiled. 'Same to you, ya bald prick.'

I watched him scurry out of the bar before ordering another soft drink. Our meeting had put me in mind of my months as a bouncer in Alice Springs and of one of the things I'd learnt there: High-Profile invited trouble. It was true there and it was true in Iraq.

In Iraq, HP was hard core. Three or four gleaming SUVs driven in tight formation like bats out of hell by clean-shaven Caucasians dressed in flak jackets and vests like extras in a *Rambo* movie was about as high-profile as it was possible to get in the Middle East. It was a dog and pony show, designed to send out a very clear warning: 'Don't mess with us.'

And, I was forced to concede, most of the time it worked. Most of the population stayed the heck away from a HP convoy. And yet, as in Alice Springs, it invited the attention of the hard men on the other side, the guys with experience, skill and cunning. The guys who knew how to fight. HP convoys were the preferred target of suicide bombers, whose mobile spotters used the simple tactic of sitting at busy crossroads or driving around looking for a fat target.

Tactically, HP and its mandatory shooting of anyone who breached the security of the hundred-metre bubble made perfect sense. But it was so 'in your face' I could see how the locals, including peaceful locals, would resent it. It was their country after all.

HP was not the way to win hearts and minds, but it was greatly favoured by most of the ex-SAS and Police Special Ops types. In fact, almost all the very experienced people preferred HP.

I went in search of Greg, finally running him to ground a few days later in the Green Zone, and asked him to schedule me for more Low-Profile operations.

He looked surprised. 'Most blokes ask to get out of LP.'

'I know, but I think it's the way to go. At least for me.' I didn't voice the moral quandary I felt about enforcing the hundred-metre bubble.

'You know what's involved?'

I nodded. 'We travel in split convoys. Different makes and models of not-very-clean, not-very-new sedans, although they're all armoured.'

'Hopefully the insurgents don't know that. Hopefully they don't notice the cars.'

'And we dress like locals. Maybe wear a flak jacket, but it's under the long shirt …'

'The *thobe*.'

'Plus everyone has a few days growth of beard and wears the headdress.'

'The *keffiyeh*, yes, that's right.' Greg gazed at me. 'Well, you could pass for a local at a distance. You're about the right height and build. Not too tall. On the weedy side.' He paused. 'Are you sure you want this?'

'Yes, I'm sure.'

'Okay. Done. It won't be only LP, but it'll be mainly what you do. We have a contract to provide security for Iraqi legislators writing the new constitution. I need men for that. You'll start tomorrow.'

***

Wearing Iraqi clothes, my body armour under my shirt, and with four days stubble and a little fake tan lotion, I could pass for a local. At least I could in the car driven by Rassim, a former Lieutenant Colonel in Saddam's army and now my guide and interpreter. Outside the car I wasn't so sure. It wasn't because I was toting an AK47 – there was nothing unusual about that in Baghdad. It was more in the way the locals moved and walked.

Most LP missions included the provision of close security on foot, accompanying VIPs from their vehicles to conferences and meetings in government buildings, hotels and private residences. I learnt the rules fairly quickly. It was not unlike watching over my kids at the beach, being always aware of where they were as I monitored the surf for rips and scanned the crowd for that one small 'something' that was out of place. Scanning the crowd … scanning the kids. Scanning the crowd … scanning the clients. Always searching for the absence of the normal and the presence of the abnormal.

But this wasn't the beach, and I was continually trying to figure out what, in this mad house, was normal. Here, what passed for normal was so far into abnormal it was totally off the wall.

Low-Profile missions were not helped by the presence of television crews, which often turned them into high-profile media events. One morning, accompanying my legislators to a conference of hundreds of delegates at Baghdad's Palestine Hotel, we were mobbed by scores of media crews just inside the lobby of the hotel. It was a struggle pushing through the crowd, and although the hotel had been turned into a virtual citadel, protected by a bulwark of T-walls and the presence of manned Humvees and Bradleys, it was still in the Red Zone and the noisy scrum was a perfect opportunity for a suicide bomber or grenade attack.

Deeper inside the hotel I felt slightly more secure. The delegates filed into their meeting room and the media drifted away while the rest of the LP crew and I remained in the lobby. Staying alert in a place with no air-conditioning and the temperature topping 100°F was not easy, nor was our role helped by the fact that the place was a functioning hotel and people were coming and going all the time.

When I noticed a young and athletic-looking Iraqi enter the hotel, my alarm bells immediately began ringing. He appeared slightly agitated, but, more questionable than that, he was wearing a jacket: an odd thing given the heat, unless he was using it to conceal a Kevlar vest, or worse – explosives strapped to his torso. He didn't approach the check-in desk, nor did he seem interested in any of the lobby shops; instead he wandered around looking, to my eyes, subtly dangerous. I asked Rassim to find out who he was and what he was doing in the hotel. When Rassim approached him the man became aggressive, whipping out a scrappy photocopy of a letter that stated he was a police officer. There was no photograph on the letter and the guy had presented no other ID.

Rassim returned and reported this as the man continued his aimless wandering around the lobby. I positioned myself on a sofa out of his line of sight, my AK47 on my knees, the safety off, my whole system keyed up and watchful for 'the move before the move' that would herald violent intent. I watched the man like a hawk, knowing with certainty that, if I judged it necessary, I would shoot him.

Deciding to shoot was relatively easy. Deciding *where* to shoot was less straight-forward. A basic infantry principle of target selection is to aim at the centre of the seen mass. If I followed that guideline I'd fire into his chest. If my target was indeed a suicide bomber I didn't like the idea of sending hot lead into packed explosives. Similarly, if he was wearing Kevlar and his intention was to use a pistol or a grenade then a bullet into his chest/vest would momentarily stun him and cause massive bruising, but it wouldn't stop him. I needed something more compelling.

As I watched, I selected my point of aim: his pelvis. He was probably close enough for a head shot, but, given the scenario, a hip shot was the better option. Not only is that target twice the size of a head, a bullet in either hip or the base of the spine would drop him instantly. Biomechanically it would be impossible for him to stay upright or mobile. Yes, a bullet in that region was definitely a more reliable option than gambling on placing a shot between his eyes.

At this point in my calculations, I was clear in my head and, most surprising of all, calm. But I also realised the utter inhumanity of the situation. Shooting to kill was one thing, but shooting to maim seemed even worse. In my heart I knew if I did shoot I'd carry a dark, possibly crippling, guilt for years to come. On a tactical level I knew the course of action was absolutely necessary.

After about twenty minutes a uniformed Iraqi policeman walked into the lobby, greeted the guy and they left together. I relaxed.

Two days later I was pointing my assault rifle at a policeman.

Rubicon

The police in Iraq worried me, as they worried many people. They were poorly paid, poorly trained and, because they were so frequently the target of insurgents, incredibly trigger-happy. It was well known that the police had a fifth-column in their ranks and that insurgents stole police uniforms and weapons to set up false roadblocks to kill or kidnap foreigners. Like most PSDs, I tried to avoid the police.

Rassim was away and I had a new driver, a young Iraqi called Tariq whom I didn't know. Returning from an LP mission I was sitting in the back seat as we travelled through the Red Zone when we were pulled over at a random police checkpoint. It was one of the disadvantages of LP missions. Rassim had always handled it well enough for us to have no hassle and to be on our way in a few moments. Tariq was not Rassim. Tariq was nervous and arrogant and soon he and the cop were in a heated argument.

I had an uncomfortable feeling and slowly eased the safety off my AK47, moving it stealthily behind the seat so I could train it on the 'policeman' without him knowing. I would need to shoot through the vinyl seat without hitting Tariq, who by now was yelling at the cop, who was angrily yelling back. Pressing the muzzle of the weapon hard against the upholstery, I carefully angled the shot so the bullet would miss Tariq's ribs and hit the cop. It was like angling a pool cue in a game of billiards – except it wasn't a game. Slowly my finger started taking up the slack on the trigger, deciding that if the cop made a move for the machine pistol slung across his chest I would fire – although I had no idea what I would do after that. The checkpoint was manned by about a dozen of these men in police uniform, and if I shot one then God alone knew what would happen next.

Luckily I did not have to find out. The cop finally stepped back and Tariq accelerated away. I breathed a quiet sigh of relief.

That afternoon a dust storm hit the city. It blew for three days and two nights, shutting down the airport and reducing visibility in the compound to less than fifty metres. The wind was neither dramatic nor violent, but it blew steadily and unceasingly, covering everything in a gritty, sand-coloured layer of dust like a light fall of snow. The dust got everywhere; in my nostrils, my eyes, my lungs, even in my mouth, although I kept it tight shut. It caked itself on my beard, my eyebrows, my eyelashes.

I noticed most of the old hands were edgy. 'Everyone seems really keyed up. What's going on?' I asked a big, gregarious, cigar-smoking, ex-Special Forces Swede I knew by his call sign, Gladius.

'The storm gives the insurgents optical cover to lay their mines. There's a much bigger risk of ambushes with IEDs after a dust storm,' Gladius told me. 'And they launch attacks under cover of the storm. In this country, dust means death. In fact there's only one good thing about a dust storm.'

I spat speckles of dust, wiping the grit off my lips. 'Yeah, what's that?'

'It sharpens you up. Makes you more watchful.'

I knew what he meant. Life, even life in Baghdad, had become routine. My days had become weeks and my weeks had morphed into more than two months, while my experience of individual convoys had blended into a memory of all convoys, just as the heat and dust of one Baghdad day had merged into a seamless memory of every Baghdad day.

What had once been extraordinary was now commonplace; the sudden chatter of small-arms fire in a nearby street, the *crump-crump* of mortar fire in the distance, the *whumping* of US helicopters overhead, the quick arching flashes of red and green rockets fired from gunships; even driving the wrong way on BIAP, although notable, failed to command an appropriate degree of respect. My system had adjusted to the mad intensity, so the adrenalin-fuelled rush of a Low-Profile mission through the streets of the Red Zone was not as sharp as it had been. Life in Baghdad had become routine. And what the big Swede, whom I respected, was telling me was that routine could kill.

It was a good reminder and I purposely psyched myself up to be more alert. It was curious; the first thing I noticed in my newly focused state was that the sounds of small arms and explosions were much closer than I'd previously thought.

I shook my head, shrugging off the notion. It could be my imagination.

In the early hours of the second morning of the dust storm I was woken by an explosion somewhere to the south, followed almost immediately by another, then another and then by the rattle of small-arms fire that went on for several minutes. It was a major action, although by whom and against what I had no way of knowing. I found out when I was having breakfast with Keith and Gladius joined us at our table.

'You hear what happened last night?'

'The explosions?'

Gladius nodded. Unusually for him, he seemed subdued. 'Insurgents stormed a compound a few kilometres from here. A suicide bomber drove a VBIED into the gates. Of course, they knew that wouldn't gain them access, so they had a second suicide bomber drive another vehicle in straight after. Then, to make sure, they drove a *third* VBIED into the gates and that did it. Four truckloads of insurgents stormed the compound and massacred everyone in it, aid-workers and PSDs.' We gazed at him, our faces betraying nothing of our thoughts.

'Only a few kilometres from here,' he repeated.

Maybe, I thought, it wasn't my imagination. Maybe incidents and explosions *were* creeping closer.

***

I was due to revert to High-Profile convoys for a couple of days. It wasn't my choice, but I was an employee and such decisions were made by other people. Sitting in my room around noon and waiting for the next mission, I was emailing Tash with the reminder that I had less than three weeks to go in Iraq when, with a roar, an enormous explosion shook the villa, rocking the walls and shaking plaster and dust down onto my laptop.

I leapt up, my chair going over as I grabbed my Kevlar vest, my AK47 and rushed out, joining the other guys crashing down the stairs. In the courtyard, pieces of twisted shrapnel speckled the ground and I could see holes in some of the roofs where shards of flying metal had punched through the tiles. Several windows were broken, the glass held together by shredded white tape hanging like bunting at a fair. Gladius was already there, standing next to the compound manager. Seconds later, Keith, the big Kiwi, charged up. 'What happened?' he gasped.

The manager ignored him and continued talking rapidly into his cell phone, ordering the compound into lockdown. I watched groups of Iraqi guards moving into position at the heavy machine-guns on the watchtowers and roofs, and

PSDs began shepherding the clients out of the exposed courtyard and back into their rooms. The big metal gates were tightly shut, no vehicles were permitted either in or out; okay for those inside, I thought; not so good for those caught on the outside with nowhere to go.

From the direction of the blast we heard a flurry of small-arms fire. Gladius stared at the compound manager, who was listening intently to someone at the other end of his phone. The manager finished and signed off. 'It's the hospital,' he growled. 'Car bomb. The place is under attack.'

The hospital was less than five hundred metres away.

'There's women and kids in there,' Gladius said.

'*Their* women and kids,' said the manager.

'Bastards.'

We stood silently in the dusty courtyard listening to the sound of machine-guns and grenades.

Unable to keep my mouth shut any longer I said, 'So what do we *do*?'

'We do what we're paid to do, and maintain security here,' the manager said belligerently.

'While women and kids come under attack in a hospital? For Christ's sake!'

'*What*, you think I *like* it?'

I backed off a little. 'Okay, okay. But we can't just do nothing. Look, there's enough of us here. I'm willing to take a fighting patrol out there to see if we can nail whoever's doing the shooting. Or, get one of the others to lead it. It doesn't matter

– so long as we do something. And if we can't kill the bastards, maybe at least we can give some emergency medical aid.'

'Don't be fucking stupid.'

'We're already fucking stupid,' Gladius chimed in. 'We're in Iraq, aren't we? How stupid is that?'

'Right, better to be stupid and useful than clever and fucking useless,' said Keith.

'No, you don't get it,' the manager said. 'You go out there without company sanction and your life insurance is invalid. You get killed or wounded and your family gets nothing. That's why it's stupid.'

We were silent, glancing at one another before staring at the ground. Although our hearts said one thing, our heads were telling us something else.

'Fuck,' Keith exploded. 'I've had a fucking gutful of this place.' He turned and stormed off, savagely kicking at a lump of tile on his way.

The heads had won.

For a moment I played with the idea of going out on my own. There were a few ways out of the compound and it was only five hundred metres to the hospital. But there was Tash and the kids. And what could one man do? Yes, that was a rational argument. Rational thinking would get me off the hook. It made inaction acceptable – no, it made it mandatory.

Rationalisation could excuse anything – including cowardice.

I sloped back to my room and called Tash on my mobile. I needed to hear her voice.

She asked how things were. 'Pretty quiet,' I lied. She was looking forward to me coming home, she told me; the kids were counting the sleeps.

I didn't sleep well that night. The guilt of not being open with Tash, combined with the guilt of being swayed by an insurance policy, played heavily on my mind.

The next day, when we heard that several women and children had been killed at the hospital I felt physically ill. Retreating to one of the bathrooms I hovered over the basin, staring at my reflection in the cracked and smokey mirror, knowing that this was not my finest hour.

That morning I was told I would be staying in the Green Zone for a few days while running High-Profile convoys. I was glad to be getting a change of scenery, if not a change of assignment: I would be escorting Iraqi magistrates to the airport and to various locations in the Red Zone.

The bullets hit on the morning of the second day, the convoy roaring through the suburbs en route to Baghdad International Airport. I felt the draught, the sudden rush of a vacuum sucking the air close to the top of my skull as I heard the vicious *crack* of a high-velocity bullet ripping open armoured metal.

I was driving the second LandCruiser in the convoy and an insurgent with a heavy machine-gun had me in his sights. The rounds had to be armour piercing, chewing through the hardened steel at fourteen hundred feet a second.

The second burst of fire was less well aimed; I watched the bitumen exploding in chunks a few feet in front of the SUV as the rounds slammed in. The third and subsequent bursts were in line with the vehicle, but low; I could hear repeated clumps of bitumen hitting my door – at least, I hoped it was bitumen.

I felt my heartbeat rocketing, my palms slick with sweat, my mouth as dry as dust.

I dropped down a gear and floored the accelerator, moderating my breathing as I swerved the big vehicle from side to side, radioing to the rear gunner in the LandCruiser ahead, giving him directions to return fire. The guy either saw something or thought he saw something because he opened up with the PKM. Every third round was green tracer, but I had no time to watch. For the next few kilometres the convoy drove evasively, madly swinging over the road before straightening up and racing for the airport.

At the airport I was still pumped, the adrenalin roaring through my system. I wasn't bothered about the return journey; in a perverse kind of way I was looking forward to it. The man who had shot at me knew his business; to hit a vehicle moving at over a hundred kilometres an hour he would have to have 'led' the target; easy enough to do in theory, but to accomplish that in action showed a high degree of expertise.

And hate. The guy had meant to do more than hit the vehicle – he had meant to kill. Me. Well, that was okay. I didn't feel any hate towards him;

if anything I admired his skill. Yet, if I got the scintilla of an opportunity, I was going to kill him. Killing the man who had tried to kill me seemed as natural as night following day. Not as an act of revenge though. My motivation was that it was the most permanent method of stopping him from trying to shoot me or anyone else.

But to kill him would require all my focus and concentration. I couldn't do that and drive at the same time, so I persuaded Sean to change places, and I rode up front, staring up at the buildings when we got to the area where the ambush had taken place. 'Slow down,' I barked.

Sean accelerated forward. '*Wit? Fackdat. Yuwannasheetdisfacker yudoitonyereenteem, bejaysus.*'

I saw no sign of my would-be assassin.

Back in the Green Zone I filled in yet another incident report before going to the Liberty Pool to swim a couple of kilometres. Afterwards, I drove to the US Prosperity camp where, in the army mess, I had a Texas T-bone, followed by a double serve of Baskin Robbins ice cream. I felt good. In fact, I felt great. I was alive.

The adrenalin turned sour and rancid in the early hours of the morning when morbid, pathological thoughts as long and as dark as a funeral procession galloped around my mind. What if the guy hadn't missed? What if, instead of killing me, the bullet had taken off a chunk of my head and left me a vegetable? What if the next round had turned me into a quadriplegic?

Prior to working in Baghdad, when I'd been developing *Leadership Without Rank*, I'd come across the Harvard Study of Adult Development. A fascinating body of research, the study provides powerful insights into what it takes to pass the most important test of all – the test of time. Over a period of 60 years researchers studied more than 800 men and women, following them from adolescence into old age, and in the process identifying clues to behaviours that translate into healthy longevity. The results of the study have not always been what even the investigators themselves anticipated.

'I had expected that the longevity of your parents, the quality of your childhood, and your cholesterol levels would be very influential,' says Dr. George Vaillant, custodian of the Harvard study. 'So I was very surprised that these particular variables weren't more important than they were.'

What turned out to be of particular importance to longevity was engagement in activity that can be broadly categorised as 'recovery' – pursuits that provide an opportunity to recharge the mind, the body and the spirit after a period of stress. Recovery is multifaceted and includes life-long learning, diet and exercise, social interaction and helping others.

On a number of levels, recovery is more important to longevity and resilience than attempting to avoid stress itself. The key to recovery is to spread the load and not become overly dependent on one particular recovery strategy. On a personal level, this principle makes perfect sense to me. Before I injured my knee parachuting, I'd run for fitness. But for me, running was about more than that, it was also how I dealt with stress. No matter what was bothering me, I'd always feel better and think more clearly after a good run. All that changed when I injured my knee. I struggled for a long time to find equilibrium before I started to discover other ways to recharge, such as reading and meditation. Those methods served me well, but in Baghdad – having recently experienced bullets fly inches above my head – it was decidedly difficult to get lost in a good book or to find solace in contemplating the Zen riddle of 'the sound of one hand clapping'.

I couldn't help thinking that the Harvard study was missing an important element. It seemed to me that something else was going on. Actually, it was obvious what was going on. I was scared.

By an odd twist of fate the mission had been my last scheduled HP convoy; in the morning I was due back on LP. Lying there in the darkness I was glad. No more HP. I settled down to sleep. I had been close to being killed, had got away with it and wasn't going to be undertaking HP any more.

But sleep wouldn't come. Something was gnawing at me. My original decision to switch to LP had been based on a tactical preference for the low-key approach. But now I found myself looking forward to it for a more visceral reason. I was suddenly afraid, and even though I knew I didn't have to do any more HP I began scheming how I could hitch a ride on a US military chopper to the airport and fly out of Iraq, ASAP. Other people had done that. Why not me?

But I knew why not.

If I did that, I would have let fear master me. Fear wouldn't stop at one thing. That's not how it works. As sick as the thought made me, I knew I had to get back on the horse. The short-term pain of facing my fear would be better than the creeping, long-term agony of letting fear control me.

The following morning I went in search of Greg. 'I don't want to come off HP just yet,' I told him.

'Yeah, why not?' he said. 'I thought you preferred Low-Profile work.'

'I do, but I'd rather stay on High-Profile for a bit longer.'

Greg gazed at me for a moment. I wondered if he would quiz me further. I needn't have worried. He had been around the track too often to start probing why people did things. People had their reasons.

He shrugged. 'Okay. Suits me.'

The next convoy on BIAP was hard to take; so was the one after that, and the next one. That night there were hundreds more 'what ifs'. The following night, after two more HP missions, there were only dozens, the night after that almost none. My mind had got tired of listening to them. It wanted to sleep. I had not conquered fear; no-one did that. But I had controlled it, at least for now.

A few days later I was ordered back to the compound in the Red Zone. Now I was ready to return to LP for the right reasons. I was also counting down the days until I went home. I had less than a week to go.

***

This time we knew about the dust storm before it hit. The forecast had said it would blow for at least three days and, in readiness, compound security was ramped up with more men crewing the watchtowers and rooftops. On the afternoon of the storm's second day we heard an explosion close by; insurgents had launched rocket-propelled grenades at an Iraqi police roadblock. The compound went into full lockdown with clients escorted back to their rooms and most of the PSDs, armed and ready, in the canteen, where there was, at least partially, some respite from the dust.

Frustrated by the inactivity and irritated by the dust, even inside, I slipped on my armour and vest, took my AK47 and stepped outside into the courtyard.

The wind, laden with dust and as hot and thick as soup, was blowing steadily, the dust reducing visibility to no more than thirty metres. I was wearing a traditional *keffiyeh*, having come to appreciate there was nothing better to cover my head and mouth during a Baghdad storm.

After a couple of minutes I asked myself what I thought I was doing. I certainly wasn't getting any fresh air.

I turned to make my way back to the canteen when I heard the boom of a single explosion, outside yet definitely close to the compound walls. I ran to the nearest watchtower and shouted up to the Iraqi lookout, 'What can you see?' I hoped his English was up to telling me.

The wind grabbed his words. I caught 'not big … one explosion … hard to see … maybe vehicle turned over.'

I hesitated. The vehicle was not one from the compound; they were all accounted for. If it had been an attack by a suicide car bomber it would have rammed the gates on the other side of the perimeter, which was the main entrance and exit. Since that hadn't happened, it might be a roadside bomb intended for a passing vehicle from another PMC. Which meant there would be PSDs out there, exposed and calling for help on their radio. In real terms they'd have quite a wait: it would take long minutes before a Quick Response Force was mobilised. And then what? Would the compound manager stand around in the courtyard and debate the efficacy of a rescue attempt like the last time? Meanwhile, what about the poor sods outside?

Against my better judgement and with a feeling of dread, I decided to do something. I had about a three-minute start on anybody else coming to the aid of anyone who might have survived the explosion.

I loped around to the least-used gate of the compound. The tertiary access point was manned by two Iraqi guards. With their focus on sheltering from the storm, they asked no questions when I motioned for them to let me through beyond the T-walls.

Outside, the world was different. It swirled dust and shimmered with hate.

I scampered close to the foot of the external wall as far as the first corner and then circled around to the parallel street.

Looking over my shoulder I could no longer see the watchtower, the dust was so thick. All I could make out was the dark outline of an SUV on its side. I moved forward with maximum caution, the metallic taste of fear in my mouth.

Insurgents often had stand-by teams ready to move into the kill-zone to execute survivors or take them hostage. If they were there and there was fighting it would be at close quarters.

Hunched low I shuffled through the dust, the sand stinging my eyes, the safety of my AK47 off, my finger inside the trigger guard.

I reached the vehicle, a Range Rover, and side-stepped around it carefully. It had taken a rocket-propelled grenade, which had thrown it onto its side. I peered down to look through the shattered windshield. The two men in the front were dead. I straightened up. The flames spurting from the engine were dying, smothered by the cloying dust. I looked around, the muzzle of my rifle following the sweep of my vision. A figure was lying in the dust on the far side of the vehicle. I scurried toward it.

A large puddle of dark arterial blood had formed around the man's hips, and despite the dust the flies were gathering. I bent to the figure, conscious of the smell of blood and cordite and burning rubber. Everywhere there was dust and filth and more dust. The man was on his side, clutching at his femoral artery, clearly in great pain.

Gently I eased him over. The face was ashen, but there was no mistaking the crooked teeth, the tombstone look, the pitted skin.

In the final heartbeats of Jocko's life I held the hand of a man who in some ways was more brother than friend. There were no profound last words. No defiant courage in the face of death. He just bled out.

***

The body of Iain Jack McKenzie was moved by truck to a US military base. His was just another name in a long list of names; casualties in something that wasn't even called a war.

Three days later I left Iraq.

I went out the same way I came in; a connecting flight to Dubai and then Qantas to Brisbane. As the plane made its big sweep out over Moreton Bay before coming in to land, I felt that surge of warmth and contentment I always felt when arriving home.

Once I'd cleared Customs and Immigration, I caught a train to the Gold Coast and from there a taxi home. It was both surreal and intoxicating to drive sedately on smooth, orderly roads lined with lush, green trees. Everything worked: the electronic tolls, the traffic lights, even the taxi's air-conditioning. When the driver complained about the traffic I burst out laughing. I kept on laughing until it became hard to breathe. That, and the taxi driver's indignant, 'What's so funny?' made me laugh even more. The perpetual pressure of living in a war zone came flooding out of me. That, and the guilt of leaving my friend Jocko in Iraq, combined with the guilt of leaving my family in Australia, rolled into overwhelming, cathartic laughter. Somewhere in the transition between uncontrollable laughter and gut-wrenching sobs, the taxi driver stopped being indignant and asked, with surprising compassion, 'Are you okay, mate?'

As far as my family was concerned, I wasn't due back until the following day. I wanted to surprise them.

When Tash and the kids arrived home from school they let out a collective exclamation of wonder at the sight of the large parcel on the veranda. It was Brontë's fifth birthday and she was the first to rush over and try to open it. She held her ground well as the older kids bustled forward, clamouring to read the notice attached to the box.

'What does it say, Mum?' they chorused.

Tash read the words out loud: 'Extreme Caution. Contains Wildlife. Open Under Adult Supervision.'

Just then a scratching noise came from inside the box, followed by a low growl.

Brontë screamed. So did her sister. Everyone stepped back from the box.

With that wonderful mix of total dread and sheer delight that young children have in abundance, one of the boys declared there was a lion inside. That theory was quickly dismissed by his brother, who knew that lions came in cages, not boxes.

When I burst out of the box I was greeted by the sight of six stunned, happy, smiling faces. I pulled Tash close to me. Then I was kissing her, breathing in the scent of her skin. There was a moment's silence before a barrage of excited children pressed in on me from all sides, enveloping me in a cocoon of laughter and life.

There was nowhere else I wanted to be.

Epilogue

There's a scene in *The Hurt Locker* where the character played by Jeremy Renner returns from Iraq to be confronted in a suburban supermarket by an overwhelming variety of breakfast cereals. It's a clever swipe at commercialism that masquerades as freedom of choice. Really, how many different breakfast cereals do we need? Or shoes? Or large screen TVs? In my case, when I returned from Iraq I didn't want to go to supermarkets. Or shopping centres. Or anywhere. It just felt incredibly good to be at home with my wife and our children. To read. To exercise. To recharge.

In adjusting to life at home after life in a war zone I decided it was time for a change, so I opened the door onto an academic path. I completed a Master of Arts, studied postgraduate law and topped it off with Executive Education at Harvard. I also decided to document elements of Kontact in a book. The end result – *Self Defence in 30 Seconds* – sold 10,000 hard copies which led to Momentum (the digital arm of Pan Macmillan) purchasing the electronic rights and making a Kindle edition available on Amazon.

The success of *Self Defence in 30 Seconds* had outcomes I didn't anticipate, including the book becoming required reading for Applied Psychology students at the Cincinnati Christian University. Another outcome I didn't anticipate was being invited to speak on Channel 7's *Sunrise*. After my first appearance, one viewer sent an email saying, 'Nice work. You were factual, realistic and the voice of reason. I assume we will never see you on TV again.' My wife thought that feedback was hilarious, and to our mutual surprise the show's producer invited me back. In the end I lost count of how many times I was on *Sunrise*, where I discussed issues ranging from stolen rocket launchers to royal weddings and the security considerations of visiting dignitaries such as Barack Obama and Vladimir Putin.

At first I accepted invitations to appear on television with open arms, not just because it was good for business but also because it's more challenging than it may seem. A live-to-air interview is usually preceded by a phone conversation and/or an email exchange with an assistant producer who dissects, in great detail, the questions that will be asked. Then, in almost every case, in the course of the actual interview the host asks completely different questions! It's infuriating, but it can be fun, thinking on your feet.

The majority of my television work was on *Sunrise*, but appearances there led to interviews on other shows, such as the ABC's *Conversations* with Richard Fidler and *Q* – the in-flight radio of Qantas, which in turn led to a 4-page feature article in Virgin's in-flight magazine, *Voyeur.*

A spin-off from the media coverage was that I was offered, and accepted, short-term security engagements in places like Jakarta, Mumbai, even Kabul. At first these engagements were relatively satisfying but over time, something unexpected happened. The subject of security no longer interested me. I simply got bored, not just with security work, but also with media interviews that focused on security. I have to admit it was nice to have strangers say, 'Hey, didn't I see you on TV?' but overall I'd rather take my dog for a walk than talk for the sake of talking. So, I kissed goodbye to the marketing benefits of media exposure and stopped accepting invitations from producers. It didn't take long before I stopped being the security go-to guy.

Stepping away from commercial security work, I focused on presenting *Leadership Without Rank* to corporate audiences. I've since spoken at hundreds of events from Ballina to Buenos Aires and beyond. It's been an enjoyable journey.

What has also been enjoyable is rediscovering an old pastime I began when I was working in Papua New Guinea. Back then, with limited access to television (and pre-internet) I filled a lot of hours learning by heart Banjo Paterson's classic, *The Man From Snowy River.*

That poem remains one of my favourites and serves as a kind of retreat when I'm bored or stressed. I don't know why it provides such solace, but I do know there is a Zen-like mindfulness in learning a poem and then reciting it from memory. Perhaps that's why better men than me have returned again and again to a particular poem they feel a special connection with. For Abraham Lincoln it was *Mortality*. For Winston Churchill it was *The Charge of the Light Brigade*. For Nelson Mandela it was *Invictus*.

When the COVID-19 crisis began to unfold I decided to record an audiobook of my ten favourite poems, called *Poetry For Men (who thought they'd never like poetry)*. It includes works from James Flecker, Percy Bysshe Shelley and other poets I admire and offers a timeless perspective on what it takes to deal with adversity.

Thanks to Booktopia's CEO Tony Nash, who helped to promote the audiobook via his *Plugged & Unplanned* podcast, *Poetry For Men* gained traction surprisingly quickly.

Emails from complete strangers who have enjoyed the audiobook rank among the most gratifying I've received. And what I find endlessly fascinating is how the same collection of poems can mean such different things to different people. For some, the poems relate to business. For others they relate to leadership. For me, the essence of *Poetry For Men* can be linked to life in general and family in particular; most poignantly, my father – who died from emphysema.

If you made a list of the ten worst ways to die, emphysema would have to be up there. Not just the dying, but all the years leading up to the last breath. The countless ambulance trips between home and hospital, the ventolin and asthma pumps and the suffocating desperation that goes with never getting enough oxygen to do even the most basic of tasks. The path leading to a total collapse of your lungs is as cruel as it is long.

I was with my father at the end, holding his hand as he tried, and failed, to take one more breath.

The only comfort I can find in his exit is that he was surrounded by people he loved, and who loved him.

I should be so lucky.

You too.

Written by Jack London and narrated by Rob Redenbach, *Call of the Wild* is available as an audiobook from Audible.